A Gift for

Logan

Presented by

Mom + Darren

Write

(Or Is That "Right"?)

Every Time

Write
(Or Is That "Right"?)
Every Time

Cool Ways to Improve Your English

Lottie Stride

The Reader's Digest Association, Inc.

New York, NY / Montreal

FOR MICHAEL O'MARA BOOKS

Editor: Elizabeth Scoggins
Illustrator: Andrew Pinder
Designer: Zoe Quayle

FOR READER'S DIGEST

U.S. Project Editor: Barbara Booth
Project Production Coordinator: Rich Kershner
Senior Art Director: George McKeon
Executive Editor, Trade Publishing: Dolores York
Associate Publisher, Trade Publishing: Rosanne McManus
President and Publisher, Trade Publishing: Harold Clarke

Library of Congress Cataloging-in-Publication Data available upon request.
ISBN 978-1-60652-341-4

CONTENTS

Introduction   8

GOODNESS GRACIOUS GRAMMAR   11

Getting Started   13
The Parts of Speech   14
How about Nouns?   15
Alternate with Pronouns   18
Further Pronouns   21
Adjectives for Extra Strength   23
Advance on Verbs   26
Past, Present, Future   30
A Regular Rebellion   38
All about Adverbs   40
It's behind You!   43
Conjunction Zone   45
Conjunction Extras   47
Oh!   48
Which Am I?   49
Building Sentences   51
What's a Clause?   54
What's a Phrase?   56
Putting Things in Order   58
The "Write" Style   59
Impressing Your Teacher   61
Bad Grammar!   64

SPELLING MADE SIMPLE 67

Spelling Things Out 68
Sounds Odd 70
Vital Vowels 71
Cool Consonants 75
Sneaky Spellings 78
Dictionary Detectives 79
Spelling Plurals 82
New Beginnings! 86
Sounds Like… 88
Good Advice 91
Sticky Endings 92
Word Games 98

PUNCTUATION PERFECTION 101

Let's Go! 102
Periods 104
Other Stops 108
For Friends' Eyes Only… 111
Comma Corner 112
Put It in a Letter 115
Punctuating Speech 117
Supercomma! 121
Conquering Colons 123
Apostrophe Alert 125
Parentheses 130
Dashes and Hyphens 131
Count on Capitals 134

INDEX 138

INTRODUCTION

Need a bit of grammar guidance? Want to be superb at spelling? Struggling with your periods and commas? Then this is the book for you. Packed with tons of helpful information, here are easy ways to remember the "rules" of grammar, spelling, and punctuation. Whether you're writing an e-mail to a friend, finishing your first novel, or perhaps one day filling out an application for your dream job, the more you understand how to use English, the better you'll do.

More Words, Please!

You probably already know that a group of sheep is called a flock, but have you ever heard of a "storytelling" of rooks or an "ostentation" of peacocks?

The English language is packed with more words than almost any other, which means there's a word for practically everything. For example, if your writing is already **s**uper **s**lick and **s**imply **s**ensational, there's a name for this style of repeating the first letter of each word—it's called alliteration. See?

How This Book Works

We have divided each section into bite-size chunks that will make tackling any part of the English language simple. You can dip in and out of the things you need help with, or read the whole book from beginning to end, with breaks, of course! If you need to look back at something at any time, there's an index at the back of the book to help you find it.

What's in Store?

Throughout these pages there are all sorts of interesting facts about the language you speak. You'll discover which countries gave us the words "pajamas" and "canoe"; that "would of" doesn't mean anything; where in a sentence a comma should go; and how to avoid accidents like this:

> If the children don't finish their vegetables, put them in the trash.

Before you know it, you'll be writing with a flourish, spelling like a champion, and punctuating perfectly, with a head full of great ways to help you improve your writing, stun your teachers, and much, much more.

GOODNESS GRACIOUS GRAMMAR

GETTING STARTED

You use grammar every time you read or write or speak. Grammar gives you all the rules about how to put words together in sentences. Using correct grammar helps other people understand what you mean.

You can make short, sharp sentences, like this:

"Get lost," she snapped.

You can be poetic:

The crafty creature slowly crept; the
terrified child shivered and wept…

And you can inform:

The two-toed sloth is a tree-dwelling
tropical mammal not noted for its speed.

Extra Information

Grammar Extra. Throughout this section, you'll find Grammar Extras that give you more detail on the subject you have just read about—these will really help you impress your teachers!

Grammar Guidance. These will give you useful tips and suggestions that will come in handy when you put grammar into practice.

Did You Know? Finally, you'll find additional information under the Did You Know? headings—interesting stuff ranging from the weird to the wonderful.

THE PARTS OF SPEECH

Every type of word in a sentence has a name, and these names are known as the parts of speech. This poem gives you a handy reminder of each of them:

> Every name is called a **noun**,
> As field and fountain, street and town.
>
> In place of noun the **pronoun** stands,
> As he and she can clap their hands.
>
> The **adjective** describes a thing,
> As magic wand and bridal ring.
>
> The **verb** means action, something done—
> To read, to write, to jump, to run.
>
> How things are done, the **adverbs** tell,
> As quickly, slowly, badly, well.
>
> The **preposition** shows relation,
> As in the street, or at the station.
>
> **Conjunctions** join, in many ways,
> Sentences, words, or phrase and phrase.
>
> The **interjection** cries out, "Hark!
> I need an exclamation mark!"
>
> Through poetry, we learn how each
> Of these make up the **parts of speech**.

The information on the following pages tells you more about these parts of speech.

HOW ABOUT NOUNS?

A noun is a name for a thing, a person, or a place. Words such as bus, chair, dragon firework, hosepipe, maggot, octopus, teacher, and tree are all nouns.

Common Nouns

There are different types of nouns, and the easiest type to spot are called common nouns. These are names for ordinary things, such as a book, a box, or a button. They are also names for less ordinary things, such as a platypus, an asteroid, or an earthquake, but they are all still common nouns. Remember, if you can put *the, a,* or *an* in front of a word, it is probably a common noun.

Grammar Extra

The, a, and *an* are short little words, but they play an important role. They are known as the definite article (the) and the indefinite article (a and an).

If you say *a* man, you are talking about *any* man. If you say *the* man, you are talking about a particular man—a *definite* man.

A MAN

THE MAN

Proper Nouns

Some nouns start with a capital letter. These are called proper nouns. They name one specific thing, such as a particular person or a particular country. Your name is a proper noun, and so is the name of the country in which you live. Here are some more examples of proper nouns, followed by the matching common noun:

Proper Noun	Common Noun
William	boy
Potter	surname
Norway	country
Friday	day
October	month

Did You Know?

The word "sandwich" is a common noun today, but it didn't start out that way. Legend has it that a tasty snack of meat placed between two pieces of bread was created for the Earl of Sandwich—Sandwich is a town in England, so it is a proper noun in this case—and named after him.

The words *cardigan, leotard,* and *silhouette* were people's names, so they were once proper nouns, too.

Abstract Nouns

The word "abstract" describes something that is an idea rather than an object. Abstract nouns are words that describe things, but not things that actually exist as objects. You can't see them or hear them, and you can't touch, smell or taste them, either.

Collective Nouns

Collective nouns describe groups of people or things. For example, a *class* is a group of schoolchildren, an *army* is a group of soldiers, and a *deck* is a group of cards.

Did You Know?

There are lots of collective nouns for animals, too. You probably know some of the ordinary ones, such as a flock of sheep or a herd of cows, but how about these particularly unusual ones?

a *business* of ferrets

an *intrusion* of cockroaches

a *descent* of woodpeckers

a *gaggle* of geese

a *pod* of dolphins

a *shiver* of sharks

a *wake* of buzzards

an *unkindness* of ravens

a *storytelling* of rooks

a *murder* of crows

an *ostentation* of peacocks

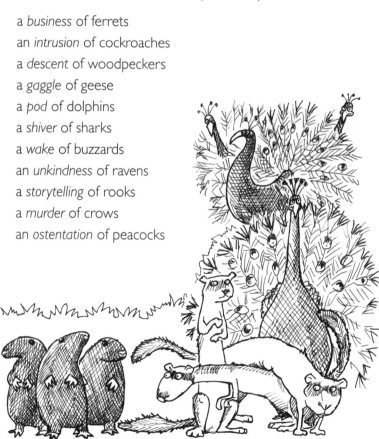

ALTERNATE WITH PRONOUNS

Pronouns are words that are used as stand-ins for nouns. This means that you can use them instead of nouns to really liven up your speaking or writing. Try reading this:

> Lucy spotted a sea monster. The sea monster had enormous horns, and the sea monster was swimming straight toward Lucy. Lucy couldn't outswim the sea monster. Could Lucy tame the sea monster or hypnotize the sea monster? The sea monster was getting nearer. The sea monster's huge mouth opened in a roar. Help! The sea monster was going to eat Lucy.... Then Lucy woke up.

This writing is a bit repetitive, isn't it? Now let's see what happens when you put some pronouns in.

Lucy spotted a sea monster. *It* had enormous horns, and *it* was swimming straight toward *her*. *She* couldn't out-swim *it*. Could *she* tame *it* or hypnotize *it*? *It* was getting nearer. *Its* huge mouth opened in a roar. Help! The sea monster was going to eat *her*.... Then Lucy woke up.

See how much snappier it is, thanks to a few pronouns? In the paragraph above, *it, she,* and *her* are all pronouns.

What's Mine Is Yours

The words listed below are called personal pronouns. The words in the first column are pronouns that you can use as the subject of a sentence. The pronouns in the second column can be used as the object in a sentence. (See page 51 for more on subjects and objects.) The third column contains possessive pronouns. These are used to show that something belongs to someone—or to several people:

Subject	Object	Possessive
I	me	mine
you	you	yours
he	him	his
she	her	hers
it	it	its
we	us	ours
you (plural)	you	yours
they	them	theirs

Grammar Guidance. Avoid using a pronoun if it makes the meaning of your sentence unclear. For example:

If the children don't finish their vegetables, put them in the trash.

Here it's not clear whether the vegetables or the children will end up in the trash!

Indefinite Pronouns

Indefinite pronouns refer to an unspecified person or thing or expresses an unclear amount, such as *all, any, none,* or *some.* Below are some of the most common indefinite pronouns:

all	everything
another	few
any	many
anybody	nobody
anyone	none
anything	several
each	somebody
everybody	someone
everyone	

Here are some sentences that include indefinite pronouns:

Everybody ran for their cars as the thunder roared overhead.

Many people chuckled at the mayor's opening line.

Anybody can join the chorus.

FURTHER PRONOUNS

Lots of different words can act as pronouns, and they have many different jobs. Here are just a few of them.

Relative Pronouns

The words *that, which, who, whom,* and *whose* can be used as relative pronouns. These are words that connect two parts of a sentence and describe the relationship between the two parts. For example:

> This is the boy *who* took my candy.
>
> There is the dog, *which* belongs to my neighbor.
>
> Where is the ball *that* I kicked over the fence?

Grammar Guidance. When referring to people, use "who." When referring to animals or things, use "which" or "that."

Reflexive Pronouns

The words *myself, yourself, himself, herself, itself, ourselves, yourselves,* and *themselves* are called reflexive pronouns. A reflexive pronoun allows you to refer back to a person or thing that you have already mentioned.

Subject	Reflexive Pronoun
I	myself
you	yourself
he	himself
she	herself
it	itself
we	ourselves
you	yourselves
they	themselves

You use a reflexive pronoun when a sentence has the same subject and object in it, like this:

I can look after myself.

In this sentence *I* is the subject, and *myself* is the object.

Grammar Guidance. Be careful. Sometimes a reflexive pronoun can change the meaning of a sentence completely:

TOM'S TEACHER WAS EXTREMELY PLEASED WITH HIM.

TOM'S TEACHER WAS EXTREMELY PLEASED WITH *HIMSELF.*

Can you tell the difference?

ADJECTIVES FOR EXTRA STRENGTH

Sometimes a noun on its own just doesn't give you enough detail—you may want to add information. To do this, you use a word called an adjective. Think of it as an added extra that describes the noun.

Using Adjectives

Suppose you need to describe a building and you want to tell people what the building is like—you'll need to use adjectives. You might say an *old, ruined* building, or a *scary, abandoned* building. *Old, ruined, scary,* and *abandoned* are all adjectives.

Grammar Guidance. An adjective goes before the noun it is describing, like this:

a *blue* moon

a *gorgeous* girl

a *grumpy* teacher

the *top* floor

an *ugly* bug

Small, Smaller, Smallest...

Some adjectives can be used to make a comparison. There are two kinds—a "comparative" one and a "superlative" one. Use the comparative when you compare *two* things. For example,

My dessert is *smaller* than yours.

A comparative adjective always goes hand in hand with "than."

You should use a superlative adjective when you are comparing *several* things, as in:

My dessert is the *smallest* of the three.

Here are some more examples:

Adjective	Comparative	Superlative
small	smaller	smallest
big	bigger	biggest
large	larger	largest
narrow	narrower	narrowest
pale	paler	palest
rich	richer	richest
easy	easier	easiest

Grammar Guidance. Adjectives that have more than two syllables (see page 71 for more on these), such as "beautiful" and "popular," do not follow the same rule. For example, there's no such thing as "beautifuller" and "beautifullest." For these adjectives you should always use the words "more" and "than" to make your comparison. For example:

Your painting is *more* beautiful than mine.

To make the superlative, you should use "most":

Your painting is the *most* beautiful of all.

This rule also works for any adjective ending in "-ous," "-ing," or "-ed," such as *famous, boring,* or *excited.*

Rule Breakers

Finally, there are a few adjectives that break all the rules. Here are a few examples:

Adjective	Comparative	Superlative
bad	worse	worst
good	better	best
little	less	least
fun	more fun	most fun
many	more	most
much	more	most

ADVANCE ON VERBS

Verbs are "doing" words. *Cry, do, go, have, laugh, like, run, skip, speak, splutter, tell, try, wish*—these are all verbs. They describe the actions of someone or something in a sentence. Without a verb, you don't have a sentence:

> Jason a mountain.
>
> Lucy her violin.
>
> Cats mice.

See? You need to add a verb for each group of words to make sense. For instance:

> Jason *climbed* a mountain.
>
> Lucy *plays* her violin.
>
> Cats *chase* mice.

Verbs in their simplest form, used with the word "to," are known as infinitives. To speak and to run, for example, are the infinitives of the verbs speak and run—you will often use an infinitive with another verb, like this:

I *like* to run.
I *want* to speak.

With or Without?

Some verbs can work well with just a subject noun (see page 58 for more on these). The following sentences make perfect sense by themselves:

Babies chuckle.
Toast burns.

However, many verbs need an object noun or they don't make much sense at all. For instance, I *buy* and I *get* don't tell you anything on their own—you need more detail:

I buy a *ticket*.
I get a *train*.

Grammar Guidance. There are lots of short verbs that you use all the time, such as *come, do, go, see, say, run,* and *walk.* However, when you're building a sentence, you can have fun thinking about which other verbs to use instead.

Not Now!

Negative words, such as *not* and *neither,* will give a sentence the opposite meaning. For example:

I *do not* want to speak.

However, two negatives in a sentence contradict each other. "I *don't* like running *neither,*" for example, means you *do* like running. This is known as a double negative and should be avoided altogether.

Lost for Words?

One of the great things about the English language is that there are so many different words you can choose to liven up your speech. How about using any of the following words in place of *speak,* for instance?

chatter
gabble
grumble
jabber
mutter
prattle
whisper

Or these in place of *run?*

bound
dash
hurtle
lope
rush
scamper
scramble

If you are ever stuck for a replacement word, try using a special kind of dictionary called a "thesaurus." In a thesaurus, words with similar meanings, or "synonyms" (see page 63), are arranged in groups so that you can easily choose an alternative word.

Know One When You See One

Words like *ring* and *hop* can be used as both a verb and a noun, so it's important to be able to identify its function within a sentence. For instance:

The phone began to ring.

The ring of the phone woke me from my sleep.

She tried to hop over the fence.

She made a short hop into New York.

In the first sentence *ring* and *hop* are used as a verb. In the second they are nouns. If you're not sure which word is the verb in the sentence, read it over and think about which word could be something a person or thing can do:

Every night I brush my teeth and jump into bed.

Which of these words can you do? Can you jump? Yes! Can you brush? Yes! Those are the verbs.

PAST, PRESENT, FUTURE

If you want to describe *when* things are taking place, it's the verb in your sentence that helps you. You can change when an action happens by changing the "tense" of the verb.

Tense Times

Tenses can tell you if something has happened in the *past*, will happen in the *future*, or is happening *right now*. You can tell your readers if a sentence is talking about the past, the present, or the future by adding a different ending to the verb, such as "-ed" or "-ing." You can also add a helper word, called an auxiliary verb, such as *will, shall,* or *am,* to help you be more specific about when the action is taking place (see pages 32–36 for more on these).

Each tense has a different name. However, these names are less import-ant than knowing when to use each form of the verb, so that what you say and write is as clear as possible.

To Be and To Have

The two verbs you use more than any other are *to be* and *to have*. You often use them to describe things or to ask questions. These sentences all use different forms of the verbs *to be* and *to have*:

I *am* cold. (to be)
She *is* tall. (to be)
Are you hungry? (to be)
I *have* blue eyes. (to have)
Who *has* my pen? (to have)

Here they are in each of their simplest forms in the present and past tenses:

(To Be)		(To Have)	
Present	Past	Present	Past
I am	I was	I have	I had
you are	you were	you have	you had
he/she/it is	he/she/it was	he/she/it has	he/she/it had
we are	we were	we have	we had
you are	you were	you have	you had
they are	they were	they have	they had

As well as acting quite happily by themselves, to be and to have also play an important role in forming different tenses, when they act as auxiliary verbs, helping other verbs to be more specific.

Grammar Extra

You are almost never allowed to say *I were* instead of *I was*, except when you are imagining or wishing a different situation to the one you are in. For example:

If I *were* rich...

Present Tense

There are two main versions of the present tense. The simple present tense uses the main verb without "to" at the beginning:

> I play tennis.
>
> You play tennis.
>
> He/she/it plays tennis.
>
> We play tennis.
>
> You play tennis.
>
> They play tennis.

Note that you add an **s** on the end of the verb when you are talking about *he, she,* or *it.*

With some verbs, such as *wish,* you'll need to add "-es" when you are talking about *he, she,* and *it:* He wishes it were sunny out.

The simple present tense can be used for all sorts of things, such as facts (you *write* neatly), and to talk about things that you do regularly (I *play* tennis).

Keep Going

To say that something is happening right now, you need the present continuous tense. This tells you that the action is taking place right now and continuing.

You use it all the time by adding an auxiliary verb—in this case, the present form of the verb to be (*am, are, is*)—followed by what is called the present participle of the verb you are using. The present participle is always made from the main verb with "-ing" added on the end:

I am *playing* tennis.

You are *playing* tennis.

He/she/it is *playing* tennis.

We are *playing* tennis.

You are *playing* tennis.

They are *playing* tennis.

Past Tense

To move the action in your sentence into the past, you can use the simple past tense.

Do this by adding what is called the past participle, usually "-ed," to the end of the main verb:

I *played* tennis.

You *played* tennis.

He/she/it *played* tennis.

We *played* tennis.

You *played* tennis.

They *played* tennis.

There are also other irregular past participles, including "-n," as in *shown*, as well as lots of irregular verbs that don't obey the rules and do their own thing (see pages 38–39).

Keep Going in the Past

You can also use the verb *to be* in its past tense (*was* or *were*) as an auxiliary verb, together with an "-ing" verb. This makes the past continuous tense, which tells you that something took place over a period of time:

I *was playing* tennis.

You *were playing* tennis.

He/she/it *was playing* tennis.

We *were playing* tennis.

You *were playing* tennis.

They *were playing* tennis.

Past Tense Extra

There are all sorts of other ways to talk about the past, too. The past perfect tense, for instance, is formed using the past tense form of *to have* (had) and another verb with its past participle. This sentence tells you about a situation in the past that was caused by something that happened earlier:

When I came home, they *had eaten* all the cake.

This tells you that there was no cake left for you, because it had been eaten.

By adding the words *used to,* you can even tell people that you once did something, but don't do it any more:

I *used to* play tennis.

This lets everyone know that you no longer play tennis.

Future Tense

Although there isn't a future participle, as there is for the present and past tense, there are still lots of ways to indicate that the action you are speaking or writing about is in the future.

One of the most common ways to indicate the future tense is to use the auxiliary verbs *shall* or *will,* followed by another verb—*play,* for instance. Traditionally, you should use *shall* for *I* and *we,* and *will* for all the other people, like this:

I *shall play.*
You *will play.*
He/she/it *will play.*
We *shall play.*
You *will play.*
They *will play.*

Keep Going in the Future

You can indicate a continuous future tense using the verb *to be* as an auxiliary verb, just as you would in the present and past tenses. This tells you that something is taking place over a period of time in the future:

I *shall be playing.*
You *will be playing.*
He/she/it *will be playing.*
We *shall be playing.*
You *will be playing.*
They *will be playing.*

Future Tense Extra

There are lots of other ways you can talk about the future, too. All you need is a selection of auxiliary verbs to help things along. For example:

I *am going to buy* shoes tomorrow.
You *will win* the race.
It *will be* sunny tomorrow.
We *shall be going* to school tomorrow.
You *are coming* with us tonight.
They *will be* here in a minute.

More on Auxiliary Verbs

You've already come across *to be* and *to have,* as well as *shall* and *will* as auxiliary verbs, but these are not the only ones. The following words can all be used to help change the meaning of another verb:

could, should, would,
do, does, did,
may, might, must

You can even combine them with *to be* and *to have* to explain a huge amount more about the verb:

I *might have been chosen*, but I was sick.

My top *could be being crumpled* since it's in a suitcase.

Grammar Guidance. What's wrong with this sentence?

I would of liked an ice cream.

That's right: *Of* is a preposition (see page 43)—there is no verb *to of*, ever. The full sentence should be:

I *would have liked* an ice cream.

This can be shortened to:

I *would've liked* an ice cream.

A REGULAR REBELLION

Some verbs, such as *to like*, are known as regular verbs. When you change their tense, it is very straightforward.

Present	Past	Future
I like	I liked	I shall like
you like	you liked	you will like
he/she/it likes	he/she/it liked	he/she/it will like
we like	we liked	we shall like
you like	you liked	you will like
they like	they liked	they will like.

However, some verbs are irregular—they don't behave as you would have predicted. Use the table on the next page to see how other verbs change from their present tense form to the simple past. You can also see each of their past participles—the words that would usually end in "-ed," as in *liked*.

Irregular Verb Table

Simple Present	Simple Past	Simple Participle
awake	awoke	awoken
be	was or were	been
begin	began	begun
bring	brought	brought
buy	bought	bought
choose	chose	chosen
come	came	come
do	did	done
draw	drew	drawn
eat	ate	eaten
feel	felt	felt
find	found	found
forget	forgot	forgotten
give	gave	given
go	went	gone
grow	grew	grown
have	had	had
hear	heard	heard
know	knew	known
leave	left	left
lose	lost	lost
make	made	made
read	read	read
run	ran	run
say	said	said
see	saw	seen
speak	spoke	spoken
swim	swam	swum
take	took	taken
teach	taught	taught
think	thought	thought
understand	understood	understood
wear	wore	worn
win	won	won
write	wrote	written

ALL ABOUT ADVERBS

In the same way that an adjective gives extra information about a noun, an adverb gives you more detail about a verb.

Take this sentence:

I eat.

This is fine on its own, but everyone eats, don't they? To give more detail, use an adverb to make it clear just *how* you eat:

I eat *quickly*.

I eat *greedily*.

I eat *slowly*.

Each of the following words is an adverb, and as you can see, a lot of adverbs end in "-ly":

angrily	jerkily	sensibly
bumpily	kindly	truthfully
cautiously	loyally	unhelpfully
dreamily	mischievously	viciously
energetically	noisily	weakly
furiously	oddly	xenophobically*
gingerly	perversely	yeomanly
happily	quietly	zanily
idiotically	rashly	

* See page 79 to find out more about using a dictionary to look up the meaning of unfamiliar words.

Grammar Guidance. Don't be tricked into thinking that all adverbs end in "-ly." Those aren't the only ones. Here are a few that you might use quite a lot:

almost	once
fast	soon
hard	twice
never	well

There are also lots of words ending in "-ly" that aren't adverbs. For example:

Hedgehogs are prickly.

The word "prickly" isn't an adverb, because it's describing the hedgehog, and hedgehog is not a verb, it's a noun. Adjectives describe a noun, remember? It's easy to confuse an adverb with a different kind of word ending in "-ly," but if you can't work out which it is, try changing the verb to see if it still makes sense:

Hedgehogs walk prickly.

This doesn't make sense, so *prickly* isn't an adverb.

Double Duty

Some words can be used as an adjective *and* as an adverb:

Cheetahs are fast.

I ran fast.

Fast is an adjective when it's telling you more about the noun cheetahs. It's an adverb when it's telling you more about the verb *ran*.

Where Did I Put My Adverb?

It often doesn't matter where you put an adverb in a sentence, because its meaning still stays the same:

She spoke *hesitantly*.

Hesitantly, she spoke.

She *hesitantly* spoke.

However, you can sometimes make some important changes if you're not careful. For instance, these two sentences have a subtle but distinctly different sense:

Idiotically, she was dancing on the cliff edge.

She was dancing idiotically on the cliff edge.

Depending on where you put them, some adverbs, such as *even, only, almost, also, just,* and *mainly,* can make changes to the meaning of your sentence. For example, each of these sentences has a slightly different meaning:

Only I gave my brother a pencil.

I only gave my brother a pencil.

I gave only my brother a pencil.

I gave my brother only a pencil.

IT'S BEHIND YOU!

Prepositions are words that show how one thing is connected to another, as in *at, by, in, of, off,* and *up.* They describe the position of things and usually go before a noun or a pronoun. For example:

> The baby was *in* the bath.
>
> The house was *by* a river.
>
> I whizzed *down* the waterslide.

You use prepositions all the time when you're speaking and writing:

> I wanted to stay *in* bed, but my mom made me go *to* school. I
> got *in* trouble for laughing *in* math class. *In* the gym I fell
> *off* the bars and went somersaulting *across* the gym. Some
> days it's just not worth getting *up* in the first place.

Sometimes a group of words can make a preposition, too:

> away from
>
> far from
>
> in front of
>
> near to
>
> next to
>
> out of

Grammar Guidance. Try to avoid using more prepositions than you need, though, such as *of* in this sentence:

> I got off *of* the bus.

The Complete List of Prepositions

about	concerning	on top of
above	despite	out
according to	down	out of
across	during	outside
after	except	over
against	except for	past
ahead of	excepting	regarding
along	for	round
along with	from	since
among	in	through
apart from	in addition to	throughout
around	in back of	till
as	in case of	to
as for	in front of	toward
at	in place of	under
because of	inside	underneath
before	in spite of	unlike
behind	instead of	until
below	into	up
beneath	like	upon
beside	near	up to
between	next	with
beyond	of	within
but*	off	without
by	on	
by means of	onto	

*But is a conjunction, unless it means "except": Everyone in the class could go on the trip *but* Sarah.

CONJUNCTION ZONE

Conjunctions are words that join things together, as in *and, or, but,* and *so.* You can join words, clauses, or phrases with them (see pages 54–57 for more on these). They make your writing flow much more smoothly. Without them you end up with lots of short sentences. Read this example:

> I met a grumpy fairy. She gave me a wish. I wished for wings. The wings appeared. They were useless. They were shimmery. They were sparkly. They were fairy-size. They were also stuck to my shoulders. "You wished for wings. You got them," snapped the fairy. The fairy disappeared.

It's a bit jerky, isn't it?

Try inserting some conjunctions instead:

> I met a grumpy fairy. She gave me a wish, *so* I wished for wings. The wings appeared, *but* they were useless. They were shimmery *and* sparkly *and* fairy-sized. They were also stuck to my shoulders. "You wished for wings. You got them," snapped the fairy *and* disappeared.

Get Coordinated!

The words *and, nor, but, or, yet,* and *so* are known as coordinating conjunctions. You use them to join words, sentences, or parts of sentences that are equally important. For example,

"Cats like to meow" and "Dogs like to bark" are equally important, so you can connect them with a coordinating conjunction, like this:

Cats like to meow, *and* dogs like to bark.

Or like this:

Cats like to meow, *but* dogs like to bark.

You can often change the meaning of a sentence with the conjunction you choose, like this:

Cats like to meow, *so* dogs like to bark.

This would mean that dogs like to bark *because* cats like to meow.

Grammar Guidance. If you are joining two sentences that contain the same noun, you can take the second noun away to avoid repetition. For example, if you join "The toddler fell over" with "The toddler started bawling" you can say:

The toddler fell over and started bawling.

Rather than:

The toddler fell over, and the toddler started bawling.

Grammar Extra

Usually, it's best to avoid starting a sentence with a conjunction, especially if you are writing a formal letter or writing an essay for English class. However, it is perfectly all right to start a sentence with *and* or *but* in stories or in informal writing. You will probably notice that lots of writers use these words for dramatic effect and for emphasis. And you can, too! It can work well, as long as you don't overdo it.

CONJUNCTION EXTRAS

Besides the coordinating conjunctions., there are three other types of conjunctions. These are:

Subordinate

Subordinate conjunctions join the more important clause to the less important clause—its subordinate (see pages 54–55). They are words such as *although, as, because, since, unless,* and *while.* For example, "I'm tired, and I slept well" can be joined together, but the fact that you are tired is more important, so the conjunction you should use is a subordinate conjunction:

> I'm tired *although* I slept well.

Correlative

Correlative conjunctions come in pairs—they correlate, which means that they compare things. They are words such as *not only… but also; either… or;* and *neither… nor:*

> He is *not only* annoying *but also* my brother.
>
> He is *neither* clever *nor* funny.
>
> He is *either* shouting *or* pinching.
>
> *Whether* I am alone *or* with friends, he gets on my nerves.

Compound

Finally, compound conjunctions are made up of more than one word, such as *so that* or *as soon as:*

> I will stay in my bedroom *as long as* I like.
>
> I am hiding *so that* he won't find me.
>
> I will come out *as soon as* they have gone.

OH!

Oh! and other words like it are known as interjections, or exclamations. They are words or phrases that appear by themselves with an exclamation mark—often as a warning or to show emotion. You might see them on signs in a safari park or near a school:

> *Elephants!* Please stay in your car.
>
> *Slow!* Children crossing.

You can use interjections in your own writing to show how someone is feeling—*Oh yes!, Wow!* They can also make great sound effects—*Pop!, Burrrgh!, Wheeeee!* Used well and sparingly, interjections can liven up your writing, but—*hey!*—do *not* overuse them. Otherwise, people may not pay attention when you use them as commands, as in, *Go!, Help!, Listen!,* and *Stop!*

WHICH AM I?

Many words in English can switch from one part of speech to another, depending on how you use them. Here's how:

Switching And Changing

Remember the verbs ending in "-ing"? These letters make up the present participle for all verbs. (See pages 30–31 if you'd like a recap.) However, sometimes words that end in "-ing" are actually nouns. They are called verbal nouns because they have been made from a verb. For example:

The *wailing* of the ghost sent shivers down my spine.

Grammar Extra

There are lots of other ways to make nouns from verbs. By adding a different ending, called a suffix (see pages 92–97), lots of verbs can be transformed into nouns. For example:

arrive becomes arri*val*

celebrate becomes celebra*tion*

inhabit becomes inhabi*tant*

Grammar Guidance. Words that end in "-ing" can also be adjectives, as in:

The *screaming* fans surrounded the limo.

The *rising* star hid his face from the crowd.

The *gabbling* presenter stood in the spotlight.

Preposition or Adverb?

Many prepositions, such as *along, before, behind, below, down, in, near, on, over, through,* and *under,* can also be adverbs. For example:

The burglar goes *up* the drainpipe.

The burglar goes *up*.

In the first sentence *up* is a preposition. It tells you *what* the burglar goes up—the drainpipe.

In the second sentence *up* is an adverb. It's telling you more about *how* the burglar goes.

Did You Know?

Some words, such as defect and reject, can be verbs or nouns, depending on how you pronounce them. (See page 88 for more on this.)

BUILDING SENTENCES

You've probably been building sentences quite happily for years, using all of the parts of speech you have read about here, so below is a quick reminder of the basics.

Nouns and Verbs

When you are writing or speaking, you always need at least two things to make a simple sentence—a noun and a verb. Put a noun and verb together, and you've got a sentence:

Balloons pop.

Birds chirp.

Boys fidget.

Girls whisper.

The noun is what the sentence is all about—it is known as the subject. *Balloons, birds, boys,* and *girls* are all nouns.

The verb provides the action in each sentence. *Pop, chirp, fidget,* and *whisper* are all verbs.

What's the Object?

Lots of sentences have an object as well as a subject. The object is also a noun, and it is the part of the sentence that the action is happening to:

Birds make *nests.*

Boys guzzle *pizza.*

Girls stroke *hamsters.*

Nests, pizza, and *hamsters* are the objects in these three sentences. The nests are being made by the birds, the pizza is being guzzled by the boys, and the hamsters are being stroked by the girls.

Me or I?

When you're using pronouns in a sentence (see pages 18–22), it can be hard to tell if you should use *me* or *I*, but use this trick and you'll soon work it out:

Imagine your aunt made lunch for you and your brother. Which of these would you say?

My aunt made lunch for my brother and *I*.

Or:

My aunt made lunch for my brother and *me*.

Leave your brother out to see which sentence works. "My aunt made lunch for I" sounds wrong, so the second sentence is right. This is because *aunt* is the subject noun of the sentence—*you* and *your brother* are the object nouns, so you use the object form of the pronoun. *Me* stands in for the object noun, and *I* stands in for the subject noun.

The same trick works in reverse, too. If you and your brother were making lunch for your aunt instead, which of these would you say?

Me and my brother made lunch for my aunt.

Or:

My brother and *I* made lunch for my aunt.

Get rid of your brother again, and you can quickly see that "Me made lunch for my aunt" makes no sense at all, so the second sentence is correct.

Do You Agree?

The verb in a sentence should always "agree" with the subject noun. This means choosing the right ending for the verb so that it matches the noun. For example, boys cannot guzzles, they guzzle, but a single boy guzzles.

This becomes somewhat trickier with collective nouns, such as pack or team (see page 17). Collective nouns can be either singular or plural, so although there is always more than one member of a team, you can either say, "The team *is* ready to go" or "The team *are* ready to go." Just choose either *is* or *are* and stick with it.

Building Extensions

Now that you know how a simple sentence is put together, here's how to build even more interesting sentences.

Take a simple sentence like this:

I threw the ball.

And turn it into something like this:

I threw the ball across the yard, and it skimmed over the bushes, past the farmyard, and landed on the horns of an astonished bull.

It's just a matter of building up an idea and adding detail. You can do this by using what are called clauses and phrases (see pages 54–55).

WHAT'S A CLAUSE?

A clause is a group of words within a sentence that has a subject and a verb—just like a sentence. A clause can make sense on its own, but it doesn't have to. For example, these are all clauses from the sentence on the opposite page:

> I threw the ball across the yard
>
> it skimmed over the bushes
>
> it landed on the horns of an astonished bull.

They each contain a subject and a verb— *I threw*, *it skimmed* and (although this one is trickier to spot), *it landed* on the horns.

Who's the Boss?

A sentence can have lots of clauses or just one, but some clauses are more important than others.

A clause that can work on its own as a sentence is called a main clause—it's in charge. A sentence can have two main clauses that are equally important. For example:

> I want pizza, and my brother wants pasta.

However, sometimes clauses are not equal. Remember the subordinate conjunctions from page 47? Words such as *after, although, as, because, if, since, though,* and *unless* are often used to join the main clause to what is called a subordinate clause.

A subordinate clause is one that doesn't make sense on its own—it's not as important as the main clause and doesn't work without one. This sentence has a main clause and a subordinate clause, joined together with the word *although:*

I want pizza, although it isn't very healthy.

The words "it isn't very healthy" don't make much sense alone since you don't know what subject they are talking about—they are a subordinate clause.

Clause Extras

You can use a clause as the subject noun or as the object noun in a sentence. For example:

That I will eat a pizza is certain.

Here, the words "That I will eat a pizza" act as the object noun of the sentence—this is called a noun clause.

You can also use a clause as an adjective to describe a noun, as in:

The pizza *that has the most toppings* is best.

Here, the words "that has the most toppings" act as a clause describing the noun pizza.

Finally, clauses can also act as adverbs, giving more detail to the verb in a sentence:

I ate the pizza *while I watched TV.*

The words "while I watched TV" give extra detail to how you ate the pizza.

WHAT'S A PHRASE?

Phrases are groups of words that are useful for adding more interest to the basic idea you are speaking or writing about. They usually don't contain a verb and don't make any sense without the rest of the sentence. For example, the phrase "left on the plate" doesn't mean anything until you see that:

There is no pizza *left on the plate*.

Types of Phrases

Phrases can get a little confusing, because there are so many types. One thing that clearly defines any phrase, though, is that it does not contain a subject and is never a complete thought. In other words, it simply can't survive on its own. Below are just a few.

The Noun Phrase

A noun phrase is a group of words that acts as an extra-detailed noun. For example:

My hungry older sister looked at me furiously.

Here, the words "My hungry older sister" are acting as the subject noun—it's more detailed than just saying my sister.

The Adjectival Phrase

A phrase can act like an adjective too, as in:

My sister, *unhappy about her empty plate*, sulked.

Here, the adjective phrase "unhappy about her empty plate" is a more detailed way of describing your sister.

The Adverbial Phrase

A phrase can do the job of an adverb, too, telling you more about the action going on in the sentence. For example:

My sister sulked *for as long as she could*.

The Prepositional Phrase

Prepositional phrases are easy to spot if you remember that a preposition is a "location" word that tells where something is, such as on, *by, as, during,* and *at* (see page 44 for the complete list of prepositions).

The prepositional phrases below begin with a preposition and are followed by a noun:

The dresses on the rack were beautiful.

The cake in the oven smelled delicious.

PUTTING THINGS IN ORDER

Choosing the right words and putting them in the right order can make a lot of difference to your sentences. Even armed with the proper tools for sentence building, it's still possible to make things unclear by accident:

The stolen treasure was found by a tree.

I saw three tigers walking around the zoo.

See? Did a tree find some treasure, or was the treasure next to a tree? And what are the chances of three tigers wandering around a zoo unsupervised? Instead, try rewriting the sentences to make more sense. For example:

The stolen treasure was found beside a tree.

I was walking around the zoo and saw three tigers.

Action!

There are two ways to use a verb. One is known as the active voice, when the subject noun of the sentence is carrying out the action of the verb:

I smashed the bottle of poison.

The other is the passive voice, when the action of the verb happens to the subject noun:

The bottle of poison was smashed by me.

The passive voice is great for signs in parks and shops:

DOGS MUST BE KEPT ON A LEAD.

ALL BREAKAGES MUST BE PAID FOR.

THE "WRITE" STYLE

When you're writing a story, you don't need to do lots of explaining right at the start—you can fill in the details later. Instead, grab your readers' attention from the first sentence:

It was raining hard the day I first met the Itchasnitch witch.

Word Order

Check your word order, too. In long sentences the most usual order is subject noun, verb, object noun, then another object noun:

The girl spotted an alien in the kitchen.

You can switch the word order so that the subject noun (the girl in this case) doesn't come first, but the sentence still makes sense:

In the kitchen, the girl spotted an alien.

OH, THE ALIEN'S EATEN ALL THE YOGURT AGAIN.

Switching the word order around can make a real difference in how your sentences sound. If your hero is struggling to push a lever and save the world, for instance, which sounds more dramatic?

The lever went down!

or:

Down went the lever!

You will also find that it helps to vary your sentence length, since a very short sentence after a few long ones will keep your readers interested. Like this. (See? Much better!)

Conversation Starters

To make the characters in your story more realistic and more interesting, add some speech. (See pages 117–120 for information on quotation marks.) A conversation between characters breaks a page of writing into shorter pieces and makes a story much more fun to read:

> "I think I'll have the last biscuit," said Davindra.
>
> "No, you won't!" Jack replied, stuffing it into his mouth swiftly.

Cutbacks

Finally, look back at what you've written. Are there any words in there you don't need or that don't add anything? If so, take them out. Look especially hard at how many adverbs you have. You might, for example, say:

> he said, grumpily.
>
> he said, excitedly.

Think about whether the adverbs really add anything. Could you show that he was grumpy or excited with the words that your character says instead?

IMPRESSING YOUR TEACHER

Here is a quick checklist of some useful grammatical terms. Throw these casually into conversation with your teachers and watch them fall to the classroom floor, stunned by your genius!

Allegory

An allegory is a story that seems to be about one subject, but it actually has a hidden meaning. It can give a message or symbolize a moral.

Alliteration

Are you a budding poet? If so, alliteration is for you. It is when you repeat a letter, usually at the start of a word, to create a feeling or an effect or to create atmosphere:

> …the low last edge of the long lone land.

Assonance

Assonance is similar to alliteration but uses repeating vowel sounds to create an interesting effect, like this:

> What noise annoys an oyster most?

Assonance can also be the repetition of consonants, as, for example, in the words *wash, wish* and *whoosh*.

Rappers use alliteration and assonance all the time, and so do advertisements—so listen carefully the next time you're watching TV.

Clichés

A cliché is an expression that is so overused that it has more or less lost its force and no longer has dramatic effect. Using clichés in writing is generally frowned upon. Here are some familiar ones:

It's raining cats and dogs.
Quick as a flash.

Hyperbole

When you are speaking or writing, you might deliberately exaggerate what you are saying to create an effect. This is called hyperbole (pronounced high-PER-boh-lee). It is a million, billion times more effective if you use it sparingly!

Metaphors

Metaphors describe a person or thing as *being* something else—they compare things for effect but aren't really true. For example:

She's a real dragon.
You're a pain in the neck.

Oxymorons

An oxymoron combines two things that contradict each other, such as:

a definite maybe
silent applause
an open secret

Paradox

A paradox is a statement that contradicts itself. For example, someone might say, "I always bend the truth," but are they telling the truth or lying when they say that?

Personification

If you are writing a story, you might give human characteristics to an animal or even an object. This is called personification. For example:

> The daffodils nodded their yellow heads.

Similes

A simile is used to compare one person or thing to another—they're easy to spot, because they often use the words *like* or *as*, as in:

> as cold as ice
> run like the wind

Synonyms and Antonyms

Synonyms are words with similar meanings. The words *enormous, immense,* and *vast* can all describe something huge. Using synonyms is a good way to avoid repeating yourself—a thesaurus is full of them (see page 28).

Antonyms are words that have opposite meanings—*big and small* or *hot and cold*, for example.

Tautology

Tautology is the combination of words with the same meaning, that form a phrase such as *free gift, short summary*, and *very unique*. It is best to avoid these.

BAD GRAMMAR!

Years ago it was considered bad grammar to "split" an infinitive—to put another word between *to* and the verb. For example:

> I am going to quickly eat something before going to the movies.

To remember what a split infinitive is, just think of *Star Trek*. This sci-fi series exhibits the most famous example of the split infinitive, right in the show's opener: "To boldly go where no man has gone before." Here, *boldly* splits up *to go*. The correct way to express this should be "To go boldly where no man has gone before." But who wants to find error with one of the longest running chronicles in TV history?

It was also considered bad grammar to put a preposition at the end of a sentence:

> What are you talking about?

Today the rules are more relaxed. Many people use split infinitives and put prepositions at the ends of sentences. Language is developing all the time—people create new words (neologisms) and phrases, such as *docusoap, e-mail* and *fashion victim,* every day. People even find new uses for old words—people *tweet* on the Internet, and computer screens have *wallpaper.*

And Finally...

Just as language moves on, so does grammar, but one thing that doesn't change is the richness of the English language. So use it well!

SPELLING MADE SIMPLE

SPELLING THINGS OUT

In some countries, spelling is a simple business. There are rules about how different sounds should be spelled, and these guidelines are always followed. However, English breaks all the rules. For example, the word *weight* rhymes with *ate,* but almost all the letters are different. Confusing, isn't it?

A Language Invasion

Over the centuries many words and spellings have been adopted from foreign languages and adapted into English.

When the Romans invaded Britain, they brought Latin with them, so many English words come from Latin, including *alien, unicorn, ignite, pavement, animal,* and *agenda.* The Vikings from Scandinavia brought Norse words—*anger, blackmail, ugly, cake,*

freckle, and *wand.* Many words, including *romance, castle, royal,* and *blue* come from French, which was spoken by Norman invaders.

Word Swipers

As if that wasn't enough, the English language has often "borrowed" words from other countries, too, such as *pajamas* and *jodhpurs* from India, *canoe* from the Caribbean, and *anorak* from Inuktitut—the Inuit languages spoken in the north of Canada.

To help with all these different spellings, you can look things up in a dictionary. That is always the best way to be sure of how to spell words (see pages 79 and 80 for more on dictionaries). However, over the following pages, you will find helpful tips to assist you in spelling all kinds of individual words and groups of words.

Read on to discover how you can become a whiz at spelling to help make your writing the very best it can be.

SOUNDS ODD

One of the strangest things about English spelling is that although most of the time you can work out how a word is spelled by saying it out loud, this doesn't always work.

In fact, more than 10 percent of the words used in the English language are not spelled the way they sound! Some of them are words you just have to learn, but there are lots of useful rules to help you, too.

Tools of the Trade

If you're reading this, you've obviously come to grips with the number one tool of the trade: the alphabet. You know that it has 26 letters and that 5 are vowels—**a, e, i, o,** and **u**—and the rest are consonants…or are they?

The letter **y** is counted as a consonant, but it's also a part-time vowel. At the beginning of a word, such as *yes* or *yacht,* it acts as a consonant; at the end of a word, such as *happy* or *silly,* it acts as a vowel. In the case of the word *rhythm,* it's definitely a vowel.

Added Extras

Spelling Extra. Throughout this section, you'll find Spelling Extras that give you extra information about the spelling rules you've just read about.

Spelling Specials. These will give you useful tips to help you put the spelling rules to good use.

Did You Know? Each Did You Know? heading will introduce an extra spelling fact that you're sure to enjoy.

VITAL VOWELS

Every word in the English language has a vowel in it some-where—and very often more than one. Each of the five vowels has two basic sounds. One is a short, snappy sound, as in *pat* and *pet;* the second is a long drawn-out sound, as in *wake* and *woke.*

The long vowel sound is spelled with what is sometimes known as the magic **e,** so that:

> hat becomes hate
>
> pet becomes Pete (short for Peter)
>
> fin becomes fine
>
> rob becomes robe
>
> cub becomes cube

Spelling Special. There are some exceptions to the rule, including the words *have, give* and *love,* which are not pronounced with the long vowel.

Spelling Extra

The magic **e** is also known as a split digraph because the vowels are sepa-rated, or split, by a consonant, but that doesn't sound like much fun, does it?

Syllables

Each part of a word with a vowel sound in it is called a syllable. The word *ban* has one syllable, and the word *banana* has three: *ba-na-na.*

I before E

Here's a well-known spelling tip you're sure to come across:

I before **e**, except after **c**,

Or when sounded like **a**

As in neighbor and weigh

This means that, as a general rule, **e** should follow **i** in words such as *piece, believe* and *field* unless there is a letter **c** before it, as in *receipt* and *receive*.

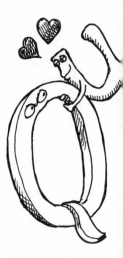

There are, however, some sneaky exceptions to this rule, such as *weird,* which also makes the long **e** sound.

Spelling Special. The letter **q** goes almost nowhere alone—it almost always has a **u** next to it, as in *quiz* and *question.* Even in the middle or near the end of a word, as in *require.*

Did You Know?

Diphthong is a funny word for sounds you make all the time, like in the words *feel* and *fail.* The vowel sound changes as you say the word aloud because your tongue moves from one position to another in one syllable.

Vowel Tips

As well as the two basic vowel sounds, it is possible to combine different letters to make other sounds, too. For example, the "aw" sound in four is made with the letters **o, u,** and **r.** Use the list opposite to spot the different ways these sounds can be spelled.

Vowel Checker

In the list below, each vowel sound has examples of the ways the sound can be spelled, with the different letters highlighted in **bold**.

A

A short "a" sound, as in hat:

c**a**t

pl**a**it

A long "a" sound, as in hate:

pl**a**te

m**ai**d

l**ay**

br**ea**k

eight

gr**ay**

g**au**ge

An "ah" sound, as in pass:

ah

h**a**lf

arm

l**au**gh

An "air" sound, as in fair:

h**air**

sp**are**

y**eah**

p**ear**

th**eir**

wh**ere**

An "aw" sound, as in dawn:

f**a**ll

t**a**lk

c**au**ght

sp**aw**n

r**oa**r

d**oo**r

sp**or**t

th**ou**ght

f**ou**r

s**ure**

E

A short "e" sound, as in pet:

y**e**t

d**ea**d

fr**ie**nd

A long "e" sound, as in Pete:

q**uay**

eke

fl**ea**

fl**ee**

dec**ei**ve

k**ey**

f**ie**ld

sard**i**ne

An "ear" sound, as in hear:

f**ear**

ch**eer**

h**ere**

t**ier**

An "er" sound, as in her:

l**ear**n

j**er**k

b**ir**d

w**or**d

j**our**ney

c**ur**d

I

A short "i" sound, as in fin:

bin

build

mystery.

A long "i" sound, as in fine:

lime

tie

sigh

dry

good-bye

O

A short "o" sound, as in rob:

wasp

sausage

spot

trough

A long "o" sound, as in robe:

hope

soap

foe

glow

An "ow" sound, as in clown:

allow

pound.

An "oy" sound, as in toy:

annoy

coin

buoy

U

A short "u" sound, as in cub:

come

young

pun

A long "u" sound, as in cube (which sounds like you):

stew

duty

Tuesday

A "u" sound, as in flute:

do

root

soup

plume

true

fruit

A "u" sound, as in bush:

look

could

full

COOL CONSONANTS

Consonants are all the letters of the alphabet that aren't vowels—except the letter **y,** which sometimes behaves like a vowel and sometimes acts like a consonant (see page 70).

Consonants can work alone, in pairs, and even in groups. For example, the letters **n, g, t, h,** and **s** don't look as if they could make any sense together, but put them in the word *strengths* and they do. (Strengths is the longest word in the English language that has just one vowel.)

Consonant Checker

Some consonant sounds can be spelled in more than one way. See how each of the sounds can be written below.

F as in four:

- **f**riend
- ga**ff**e
- cou**gh**
- **ph**oto

G as in great:

- **g**o
- e**gg**
- **gh**oul
- **gu**ess

J as in jellies:

- **j**olly
- e**dge**
- **g**igantic

K as in kites:

- **k**ick
- **c**ount
- a**cc**ount
- e**ch**o
- blo**ck**
- bou**qu**et
- pla**que**

S as in sooner:

- **s**aid
- ni**c**e
- **sc**ience
- ki**ss**

"Sh" as in shoes:

- **sh**opping
- ma**ch**ine
- so**c**ial
- **s**ugar
- ten**s**ion
- a**ss**ure
- posse**ss**ion
- men**t**ion

Y as in yapping:

- **y**ou
- **u**se

Z as in zoo:

- **z**ip
- dai**s**y

Soft, Soft, Soft

The letters **c** and **g** both have two different sounds—one hard, as in the words *cold* and *gold;* one soft, as in *cell* and *gel*. The letters **c** and **g** are usually soft whenever they are followed by the letter **e, i,** or **y.** For example:

saucer and germ

decide and giant

gymnast and cylinder

Some words, such as *circus* and *garage,* have both the hard and the soft sounds in them.

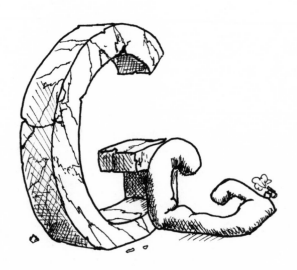

Consonants And Suffixes

Adding a new ending to a word is known as adding a suffix (see pages 92–97). You sometimes need to double the consonant at the end of the word. This happens when:

- the word has one syllable.
- the word ends in a single consonant following a vowel.
- the suffix—or word ending—begins with a vowel.

For example:

flat becomes fla*tter*

nod becomes no*dding*

tap becomes ta*pped*

Doubling the consonant makes sure that the vowel sound stays the same when you add your suffix. This is easy enough in short one-syllable words, but in longer words you need to listen to how they are pronounced to decide whether you need to double the consonant or not.

When you say a long word aloud, usually you stress, or emphasize, a particular part of the word. For example, when you say the word *enter,* you stress the first syllable. But when you say the word *prefer,* you stress the second syllable. This means that when you are adding a suffix, you need to double the letter **r** at the end of the word *prefer,* but you don't need to double it at the end of *enter:*

enter becomes ente*red* and ente*ring*

prefer becomes prefe*rred* and prefe*rring*

SNEAKY SPELLINGS

Some spellings are extra sneaky. Words that contain the "ough" spelling can make all these different sounds:

cough, which rhymes with off
bough, which rhymes with ow
though, which rhymes with oh
thought, which rhymes with aw
through, which rhymes with ooh
tough, which rhymes with uff

Not so long ago, it was even used to make an "up" sound, when *hiccup* was spelled *hiccough*. The new spelling is much more sensible.

One-and-Only Words

Some spellings are one-offs—words you just have to learn because there's no way of guessing how to spell them from their sound. Here are three to begin with:

beauty
biscuit
moustache

Did You Know?

The famous scientist Albert Einstein, who developed theories about time and space, was a genius, but even he found spelling quite tricky.

DICTIONARY DETECTIVES

It's important to get to know how to use a dictionary, whether it's to check your spelling or to look up the meaning of a word you're stuck on.

Know Your ABCs

Since you already know the order of the alphabet, you're well on your way to being able to use a dictionary, because that's how dictionaries are organized. Words beginning with **a** are followed by words beginning with **b,** which are followed by words beginning with **c,** and so on.

What happens if two words begin with the same letter, though? Would you find *type* before or after *tape*? If two words begin with the same letter, the dictionary uses the second letters to put them in order. Whichever comes first in the alphabet comes first in the dictionary:

tape comes before type

If the second letters are the same, the third letter is used to figure them out: so *tame* comes before *tape*. This goes on until a letter that's different crops up. For example:

truce comes before truck

No Trouble

If you haven't got a clue how to spell a word—*trouble,* for example—try saying it aloud. You might guess quite closely with "trubble" or "trubbel," but you might guess something like "chrubble." When a word is nowhere to be found in your dictionary, try asking yourself the questions that follow on the next page.

- What sound can I hear at the start of the word?
- Am I sure I've got it right with "chr"?
- What other ways could that sound be spelled?

You can also use the Consonant Checker list on page 75 to narrow down what the first letter might be. Once you've worked out the beginning of a word, use the Vowel Checker list to help you spell the next sound (see pages 73 and 74).

Silent Letters

Occasionally, you might find that you have trouble figuring out the first letter of a word because…*shhh!*…it's silent! Here are some examples that you're likely to come across:

g as in gnash, gnat, and gnome

h as in honest, hour, and heir

k as in knee, knob, knot, and knife

p as in psychology, pneumonia, and pterodactyl

w as in who, whole, wrong, and write

SHHH!

Spelling Special. Lots of silent letters always come hand in hand with a particular letter or letters. For instance, a silent **k** is only ever before the letter **n;** a silent **p** is always before **n, s,** or **t;** a silent **w** is always before the letters **h** or **r.**

More Silent Letters

There are also words that have a silent letter in the middle or at the end. Even though you can't hear them, you still need to write them out. Here are some of the most common ones to watch out for:

b as in comb, lamb, thumb, debt, and subtle

g as in design, resign, and sign

h as in rhinoceros, rhubarb, rhyme, what, when, whee, whip, white, and why

l as in calm, half, talk, and walk

n as in autumn, condemn, hymn, and solemn

s as in aisle and island

t as in castle, listen, rustle, and whistle

w as in sword and answer

Spelling Special. The letter **e** on the end of words usually isn't pronounced—as in, for example, *tape* and *hope*.

Did You Know?

Silent letters weren't always silent. Until Shakespeare's time, for example, the **k** in knight was still sounded out. Gradually, the way these words are pronounced has changed, but the spellings have stayed the same.

SPELLING PLURALS

A singular noun tells you there's just one of something—an apple or a cat, for instance. Plurals are nouns that tell you there is more than one of something, as in apples and cats.

Plural Endings

Most of the time, you make a plural by adding a letter **s** to the end of a word. However, there are lots of words where this doesn't work—just try to say *witchs* or *wishs* and you'll see why. For words that end in "-ch," "-sh," "-ss," "-tch," "-x," or "-z," you'll need to use "-es" instead of just "-s" to make the plural. *Witches* and *wishes* are much easier to say!

Here are some other examples:

arch becomes arches
bush becomes bushes
pass becomes passes
watch becomes watches
fox becomes foxes
klutz becomes klutzes

Plurals Checklist

Y Endings. If the letter before the **y** is a vowel, as in day, put an **s** on the end:

day becomes days

If the letter before the **y** is a consonant, as in *trolley,* drop the **y** and add "-ies," so:

trolley becomes trollies

The only time you don't do that is with names, because they always stay the same:

The Kennedy family lives next door.

The Kennedys live next door.

F Endings. If a word ends in two **f**'s, as in *cliff,* you simply add an **s** to make cliffs. However, for words that end in a single letter **f**, or the letters **f** and **e,** you need to drop the **f** and change the ending to "-ves" to make the plural, as in:

elf becomes elves

knife becomes knives

leaf becomes leaves

life becomes lives

Spelling Special. There are a few exceptions to the **f**-ending rule—these words don't take the "-ves" ending when you make the plural:

belief becomes beliefs

chief becomes chiefs

roof becomes roofs

O Endings. Unfortunately, there's no fixed rule for words that end in the letter **o.** Their plurals either end in just "-s" or "-es." It's worth learning these:

echoes

heroes

mosquitoes

potatoes

tomatoes

Weird Plurals. Some words are quite different when they become plurals. These are worth remembering:

child becomes children

mouse becomes mice

goose becomes geese

Plurals of Hyphenated Words. Some nouns are made up of two or more words joined by hyphens. These are called hyphenated nouns. Most of the time you can simply pop an **s** on the last word to make the plural, but there are some exceptions. For example, in the word *sister-in-law, sister* is more important than *law,* so it becomes *sisters-in-law.*

When in Rome. Remember how a lot of English words came from Roman invaders? Well, they left their Latin plurals here, too, and some words still work happily with Latin endings as well as with "-s" endings. Latin word endings work like this:

-a changes to -ae, so antenna becomes antennae*

-is changes to -es, so axis becomes axes

-us changes to -i, so hippopotamus becomes hippopotami*

-um changes to -a, so medium becomes media

* However, antennas and hippopotamuses are also accepted ways of spelling these two words.

84

Did You Know?

Some words, such as *deer, moose,* and *sheep,* stay the same—whether you have one sheep or a whole flock of sheep. The plural of *fish* can be *fishes* or just *fish,* but some words, such as *trousers,* are always plural and don't have a singular at all. These include:

clothes

glasses (that you see through)

pants (as in underwear)

scissors

shorts (that you wear)

NEW BEGINNINGS!

You can add to the beginning of a word using what's known as a prefix. This is a letter or group of letters that change the meaning of the main word. "Pre-" itself means before or in front, which might help to remind you what a prefix is.

Prefix Checklist

You can often work out the meaning of a word that has a prefix attached to it if you have an idea of what the prefix means. Here are some you'll come across frequently, with some examples of words that they appear in:

ab-	away, from	*ab*sent and *ab*stract
ad-	toward	*ad*vance and *ad*vantage
anti-	against, opposing	*anti*climactic and *anti*septic
de-	from, out, down	*de*part and *de*scend
ex-	out of, away from	*ex*it and *ex*tract
extra-	outside, beyond	*extra*ordinary and *extra*terrestrial
inter-	between, among	*inter*national and *inter*view
intra-	within, inside	*intra*venous and *intra*mural
mal-	bad, wrong	*mal*ign and *mal*practice
re-	back, again	*re*do and *re*appear
semi-	half	*semi*circle and *semi*private
sub-	below, under	*sub*marine and *sub*standard
tele-	far off	*tele*scope and *tele*port

Topsy-Turvy

Prefixes, such as "dis-," "il-," "im-," "in-," "ir-," "mis-," and "un-," change words so completely that they give them the opposite meaning, so that:

obey becomes *dis*obey
logical becomes *il*logical
possible becomes *im*possible
attentive becomes *in*attentive
regular becomes *ir*regular
behave becomes *mis*behave
interesting becomes *un*interesting

Spelling Special. The main word and the prefix always keep all their letters, even if two of the same letters end up joined together, as in *natural* and *unnatural*. (Plus, of course, *spell* and *misspell!*)

Extraspecial

Some prefixes, such as "super-," add to the meaning of a word, so that a *hero* becomes a *superhero*. Super comes from a Latin word meaning above, so a superhero is better than a normal hero.

SOUNDS LIKE...

There are quite a few words in English that sound alike but aren't spelled the same or have the same meaning. For example, *knot* and *not*, and *whole* and *hole*.

These words, and others like them, are known as homophones. Here are some of the ones you're most likely to come across:

allowed and aloud	read and reed
beach and beech	right and write
boy and buoy	sail and sale
fair and fare	their and there
hear and here	too and two
know and no	wear and where
pale and pail	weather and whether
passed and past	which and witch
plain and plane	wood and would

Spelling Special. In words such as *it's* and *its* and *who's* and *whose*, apostrophes can cause a homophone headache. Turn to page 125 to find out more about them.

Boing! Boing!

There's a whole group of words that try to get as close to a real-life sound as they can. The words *sizzle, slap, slurp, smash, snap, splutter, swish,* and *swoosh* are all using what is called onomatopoeia (pronounced on-uh-mat-oh-*PEE*-ya). This is when words spell out the way that something sounds.

Things click and things crackle; things go kerplunk and kerching. Horses clip-clop and clocks tick-tock. Corks pop, cars vroom and rockets zoom. Children who catch colds go "Atishoo!" and toddlers who fall go "Boo-hoo."

Then there are animal noises too:

buzz

heehaw

meow

oink

quack

squawk

squeak

twitter

woof

Heteronyms

These are words that are spelled the same, have different meanings, and are also pronounced differently. For example, *does*, when it rhymes with *buzz*, is part of the verb *to do*, but when it rhymes with *froze*, it means more than one female deer!

Homographs

These are words that are spelled the same but that have different meanings. For example:

I gave a friend a *present*.
I had to *present* my project to the class.

The film left a *tear* in my eye.

I couldn't *tear* myself away.

The *wind* blew the wash away.

I helped my aunt *wind* her wool.

Spelling Special. Sometimes homographs are pronounced differently when they have different meanings. For example, a *rebel*—with the stress at the beginning of the word—is a person who *rebels*; to *rebel*, with the stress at the end of the word, is a verb meaning to disobey the rules. You need to read the sentence that words like these appear in to decide which meaning is meant and which way it should be said.

Did You Know?

Other languages use onomatopoeia, too. English cats purr, French cats go ron-ron, and German cats go schnurr.

Invent-a-Word

You can have a lot of fun with onomatopoeia, inventing new words for any kind of sound. The beauty of it is this: You can be as adventurous with your spelling as you like—and no one can tell you it's wrong.

What noise does a toaster make when it pops up? *Pdung,* maybe? Or how about the sound of nails scraped down a blackboard? *Skrercccch?* And how would you spell the sound of water going down a drain?

GOOD ADVICE

Some words, such as advise and advice, are easy to confuse because they sound very similar. With a **c** it is a noun (advice), and with an **s** it is a verb (advise)—remember that the letter **c** comes before the letter **s** in the alphabet and that the word noun comes before the word verb in the alphabet, too.

Quite a few other words are easy to confuse, but putting them in a sentence often helps. Try these two:

I accept your invitation.

Everyone was invited except me.

Accept means to take something or say yes—if you were invited to a party, for example. Except means to leave out.

STICKY ENDINGS

A suffix is a word ending, such as "-ed," which makes the past tense, and "-ly," which often makes an adverb. A suffix is added to a word to make the word work in a different way. For example, the suffixes "-hood," "-ish," and "-like" can be added to *child* to make *childhood, childish,* and *childlike.*

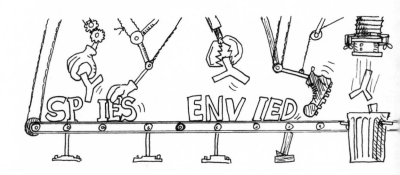

No End of Suffixes

There are lots and lots of suffixes you're sure to come across. Many words, just like *child,* can happily use different endings to change their meaning.

There's cap*able*, compli*ance*, pleas*ant*, comment*ary*, hibern*ation*, pati*ence*, independ*ent*, bak*ery*, hope*ful*, beauti*fully*, hor*rible*, wish*ing*, a*rise*, sel*fish*, hero*ism*, speech*less*, life*like*, love*ly*, amuse*ment*, strange*ness*, direct*ory*, danger*ous*, proced*ure*, and many, many more!

Suffixes Checklist

E Endings. For words that end with the letter **e,** take a look at the suffix—if it begins with a vowel, as in "-ation," "-ing," and "-ism," drop the **e,** then add the suffix. For example:

imagine (imagin -ation) imagination

pounce (pounc -ing) pouncing

favorite (favorit -ism) favoritism

However, if you are adding the suffix "-ing" to a word ending in the letters "-ie," as in *lie* and *tie*, replace those letters with the letter **y** before tacking on "-ing." Otherwise, you'll get *liing* and *tiing* instead of *lying* and *tying!*

Y Special. For words that end in the letter **y** (the part-time vowel), the rule can vary. If the letter before the **y** is a consonant, as in *envy* and *sticky,* replace the **y** with an **i:**

envy becomes envied and enviable

sticky becomes stickier and stickiest

If the suffix starts with the letter **i,** as in "-ing," keep the **y:**

envy and envying

You also need to keep the **y** if the letter before it is a vowel:

pay and paying

annoy and annoyance

Spelling Special. One-syllable words that end in **y,** such as *spy* and *cry,* have their own rule. Keep the **y** ending unless you are adding the suffixes "-ed" or "-es."

> spy becomes spied or spies
>
> cry becomes cried or cries

The letter **y** can be a suffix all by itself when it is making words such as *pimply* and *simply.* In these kinds of words, the part-time vowel takes the same rule as other suffixes starting with a vowel—drop the **e** and add the suffix "-y":

> pimple (pimpl -y) pimply

Rule Breakers

For words that end in two **e**s, a **y** and an **e,** or an **o** and an **e**, you need to keep the letter **e** when you are adding a suffix. For example:

> flee becomes fleeing and flees
>
> eye becomes eyeing and eyes
>
> toe becomes toeing and toes

Even the rule breaker has a rule breaker, though. If you are adding the suffix "-ed," remove the letter **e** so that:

> flee becomes fled
>
> eye becomes eyed
>
> toe becomes toed

For words such as *peace, singe,* and *outrage,* you must keep the letter **e,** or the **c** and **g** sounds become hard instead of soft. So:

> peace becomes peaceable
>
> singe becomes singeing
>
> outrage becomes outrageous

Spelling Special. Keep the **e** in words such as *dye* so that you don't muddle *dyeing* and *dying!*

Odd Ones Out. When you are adding the suffix "-ous," there are some words in which you need to take out the **e** even if it isn't at the end of the word. These include the words *disaster, monster,* and *wonder.* So:

> disaster becomes disastrous,
> not distasterous
>
> monster becomes monstrous,
> not monsterous
>
> wonder becomes wondrous,
> not wonderous

L Words. For words that end in the letter **l,** preceded by a single vowel, simply add "-ed" or "-ing." The same goes for two vowels, as in wheel:

> traveled and traveling
> wheeled and wheeling

When you are describing something as full—full of joy or full of care, for instance—add the suffix "-ful" to the word, but make sure you drop the last **l:**

> joy and full becomes joyful
> care and full becomes careful

However, when you add the suffix "-fully" to a word, make sure that you keep the double **l.** For example:

joyfully and carefully

Other Doubles. If the main word has one syllable and the suffix begins with a vowel, double the consonant. So:

dig becomes digging

hot becomes hotter

For longer words, say the word aloud and listen to where you stress the word. If you stress the first syllable, as in ENTer, you don't double the consonant. If you stress the second syllable, as in adMIT and beGIN, you do double:

admit becomes admitting

begin becomes beginning

If the word ends in two vowels before a consonant or if it ends in two consonants, you don't need to double:

peel becomes peeling

stick becomes sticking

Possible or Possable? The suffixes "-able" and "-ible" sound similar, but there are ways to tell them apart. The suffix "-able" often has a hard-sounding **c** or **g** before it, as in:

applicable and huggable

The suffix "-ible" often has a soft-sounding **c** or **g** or a hissing **s** sound in front of it, as in:

legible and possible

What's the Difference? The suffixes "-ance" and "-ence" can turn verbs into nouns. For example, *difference* from *differ.* Verbs that end with the emphasis on a single vowel followed by **r** always use the suffix "-ence" to make a noun:

occur becomes occurrence

prefer becomes preference

Is It Important? Words ending in "-ant" and "-ent" are often adjectives. Their spelling matches their nouns, so it's:

abundant and abundance

entrant and entrance

different and difference

excellent and excellence

Stationary or Stationery? Don't confuse *stationary,* which means not moving, with *stationery,* which means things like pens, paper, and envelopes. Remember that station*e*ry has a letter **e** in it, just like the words pen and envelope.

Did You Know?

Supersede is the only word that ends in "-sede"—all the other words that end in the same sound, such as *precede* and *proceed,* are spelled "-cede" or "-ceed."

WORD GAMES

Once you're comfortable with spelling and all of its rules, there are some fun ways to play around with the English language.

Anagrams

An anagram is when you take the letters of one word or a group of words and turn them into something different. For instance, the word *carthorse* has the same letters as the word *orchestra*.

The best anagrams make a related word or phrase (sort of!) from the letters of the first word or words, like these:

schoolmaster—the classroom

the Morse Code—here come dots

William Shakespeare—I am a weakish speller

Why not try creating some yourself?

Palindromes

You could also try palindromes—words that are spelled the same way forward and backward. *Eye, deed, level, noon, pip, pop,* and *toot* are all palindromes. You can make them from whole sentences, too. For example:

Don't nod.

Was it Eliot's toilet I saw?

Never odd or even.

Did You Know?

A man named William Archibald Spooner was known for

accidentally switching the beginnings of words around as he spoke. These mistakes became known as spoonerisms. For example, if you mean to say, "Stop flipping the channel!" but instead say, "Stop chipping the flannel!" this is a spoonerism. It can happen all the time, especially if you are in a rush, or nervous, like William Spooner.

a crushing blow—a blushing crow

a pack of lies—a lack of pies

it's pouring with rain—it's roaring with pain

you have bad manners—you have mad banners

a half-formed wish—a half-warmed fish

lighting a fire—fighting a liar

blow your nose—know your blows

save the whales—wave the sails

And Finally...

A great way to get the hang of spelling is to read and read and read. You can read anything—the backs of cereal boxes, comics, game instructions, your sister's secret diary (okay, maybe not that one). It all helps.

The more you read, the more that words and their spellings sneak into your brain. So have fun with spelling— and read as much and as often as you can!

PUNCTUATION
PERFECTION

LET'S GO!

Take a look at these paragraphs. Which one do you think has the right punctuation?

This one:

> The house looked deserted. Empty. I pushed open the door. "Hello," I called. Silence. No one answered. Just then, I heard a noise. Crrrrrrk. A floorboard. Then... footsteps!

Or this one:

> The house looked deserted, empty. I pushed open the door. "Hello?" I called. Silence; no one answered. Just then, I heard a noise—*crrrrrk*—a floorboard. Then footsteps.

Actually, they both are. This is because, although there are rules you need to learn, punctuation does give you options, so there's no need to panic over semicolons and commas.

The important thing is to use punctuation to make your writing clear. The marks you use give extra information about your writing, like leaving a trail of clues for your reader. They help to show exactly what you mean.

Added Extras

Punctuation Extra. Throughout this section, you'll find Punctuation Extras that give you extra information about the spelling rules you've just read about.

Punctuation Pointer. These will give you useful tips to help you put the punctuation rules to good use.

Did You Know? You'll find an extra punctuation fact you're sure to enjoy under each Did You Know? heading.

A Trail of Clues

When you speak, you give lots of clues to help people understand what you're saying. You raise and lower your voice; you leave long and short pauses; you use gestures—all to help another person understand what you are saying. That's what punctuation does when you are writing.

A simple change of punctuation can convey a lot of things about your tone of voice, too. Suppose a friend looked at your outfit for an important occasion and gushed:

"That's your best outfit ever!"

You'd be pleased, confident, ready to go—but if he or she looked at your outfit and said, in a questioning tone:

"That's your best outfit ever?"

You'd probably get changed! One little mark on the page can have the same effect. That is the magic of punctuation.

PERIODS

A period might not be much to look at, but don't be fooled. It does a huge amount for such a small dot. The most important thing a period does is to tell you when a sentence is finished; otherwise, this happens:

> It was a bright, sunny day there wasn't a cloud in the sky in just a few hours I'd be on a train in a few more hours I'd be putting up the tent with Dad we had a whole week of camping ahead

Try reading it aloud. It's hard, isn't it? Everything's confused. None of it makes sense, and you run out of breath. If you put in some periods, it's a completely different matter:

> It was a bright, sunny day. There wasn't a cloud in the sky. In just a few hours, I'd be on a train. In a few more hours, I'd be putting up the tent with Dad. We had a whole week of camping ahead.

The periods tell you where to pause. They give you time to take in the meaning of a sentence and gather your breath before reading the next sentence.

Punctuation Pointer. Sentences always start with a capital letter. See pages 134–137 for more on capitals.

Abbreviations

Periods can be used for jobs other than for ending sentences. When you shorten a word, it's called an abbreviation—such as *Mon.* for *Monday* or *Tues.* for *Tuesday*. The period at the end shows that the word has been shortened, although it is becoming more and more common not to bother with the period.

There are times, though, when it's a good idea to use periods to make things clear. Here are two you will often use:

> I went to bed at 9:00 P.M. last night.
> I got up at 7:00 A.M. this morning.

When an abbreviation could be confused with another word—A.M. and am, for example—it's important to make things as clear as possible.

Did You Know?

The abbreviations A.M. and P.M. come from the Latin words *ante meridiem* (before midday) and *post meridiem* (after midday). Use periods for both of them.

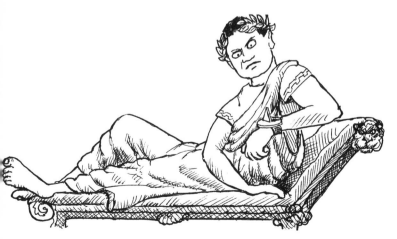

Contractions

Contractions are words that are shortened by keeping the beginning and end but taking out the middle:

Dr. is short for doctor

Mr. is short for mister

Mrs. is short for missus

People often use periods at the end of these words to show that the words have been shortened, but more and more the period is being omitted.

You may also frequently see the abbreviation *no.* It is a contraction that comes from the Latin word *numero,* meaning number. In this case, you need to use a period to make it clear that you don't mean the word *no:*

Rule No. 1: no midnight feasts

Rule No. 2: no jumping on furniture

Punctuation Pointer. If your sentence ends with an abbreviation, you don't need to add an extra period. So it wouldn't be:

I went to bed at 9:00 P.M..

It would be:

I went to bed at 9:00 P.M.

Don't Stop These

An acronym is a word that is formed from, or based on, the initial letters or syllables of a group of words (see page 71 for more on syllables). You don't need to put periods between each letter.

Lots of acronyms use capital letters:

POW—Prisoner of War

UFO—Unidentified Flying Object

USA—United States of America

Some acronyms don't use capital letters and are used as nouns. For instance, a **l**ight **a**mplification by **s**timulated **e**mission of **r**adiation is actually a laser; **ra**dio **d**etection **a**nd **r**anging is called radar; a **s**elf-**c**ontained **u**nderwater **b**reathing **a**pparatus is usually known as scuba gear.

OTHER STOPS

There are two other ways to end a sentence, apart from using a period—a question mark (**?**) and an exclamation point (**!**). Here are some examples:

Are you coming to the park?

Let's go on the swings!

Is That a Question?

Sentences that are questions are usually shown with a question mark at the end. Spotting when you need to use a question mark is easy when the sentence uses a question word like these:

Who? What? Where? When? Why?

Or when it is a longer, direct question, like these:

How did you do that back flip?

What made you think you could eat three pizzas?

Who scribbled hearts on the cover of my journal?

However, it isn't always that easy to spot a question. Some are sneaky. They start off like normal sentences:

It's not raining.

You like watching TV.

But if you tag a bit on the end—hey, presto—they turn into questions:

It's not raining, is it?

You like watching TV, don't you?

Are You Asking or Telling?

Some sentences look as if they should have a question mark, but they actually don't require one, like these:

He asked if he could leave the table.

The question is whether it's sunny enough for a picnic.

These are known as indirect questions. They describe a question, but they don't actually ask it. To spot an indirect question look out for words such as ask or wonder, often followed by if, when or whether.

The following sentences each contain the question words (when, where, and why), but they're not questions, either:

I couldn't decide when to do my homework.

I don't know where my ruler is.

I wonder why he left so soon.

Punctuation Pointer. If a question ends in an abbreviation (see page 105), such as A.M. or P.M., this question mark still needs to be added:

Do you mean 3:00 P.M. or 3:00 A.M.?

Exclamation Points!

You should use an exclamation point to highlight a word, phrase, or sentence (or for interjections—see page 48). Exclamation points are a useful way of indicating all kinds of emotions, such as happiness, fear, surprise, or pain.

Using exclamation marks in speech shows a shout or a yell. Putting one on the end of words such as *Ouch!* and *Oh!* adds emphasis to what your characters are saying.

If you want to show that someone is bellowing out orders, "Sit down!" has much more impact than "Sit down."

You can use exclamation points to show sound effects, too—
Zzzzz!, *Whoosh!*, *Zoom!* These words will make even the comic
strip below more exciting:

Watch out, though. It's very easy to go too far with exclamation points—using them too often can even come across as
SHOUTING:

> "Stop!" shouted the woman. It was no good!
> The naughty monkey ran off with her hat!

See? Exclamation points really leap off the page, so if you put
in too many, your reader will find it distracting or even annoying, since it's a bit like laughing at your own jokes.

Punctuation Pointer. Think of punctuation marks as a team.
Make the exclamation mark sit on the bench most of the
time. Only use it when your period really needs replacing.

FOR FRIENDS' EYES ONLY...

There's a difference between writing for your teacher and writing to your friends. Here are some handy ways you can use exclamation points in casual writing, but remember, they're not for schoolwork:

My brother dyed his hair purple (!) today.

Tucking away the exclamation mark in brackets shows what you think. It's a sly little comment regarding what you've written.

How about an interrobang? An interrobang is a question mark and exclamation mark combined, like this: ?! Your teachers will tell you that a sentence cannot have more than one ending— and they're right—so only use this one between friends. It's a fun way of showing that you're astonished and baffled at the same time:

My sister wants more homework. Can you believe it?!

Remember not to go overboard, though. Even your best friends will be gnashing their teeth—or snoring—by the time they get to the end of something like this:

Hi! Thanks for the invite! I'll get there early—so be up!!! Did you decide to invite Keisha after all?! Will she bring Ella?! I hope not! Who else is coming? I need to know!!!

COMMA CORNER

The comma (**,**) is a tiny mark that packs a punch. It tells you where a sentence needs a short pause, it separates items in a list, and it splits a sentence into phrases and clauses (see pages 47–49 for more on these).

Comma Power

By moving, adding, or taking away a comma, you can change the meaning of a sentence completely. A comma in the wrong place can make things very confusing. You could say:

My favorite foods are fish eggs, and potato chips.

Or you could say:

My favorite foods are fish, eggs, and potato chips.

The first sentence will make everyone think that the eggs that fish lay are one of your favorite foods. That's perfectly fine if they are, but if fish eggs are the last thing you'd like for lunch, then you need to think carefully about where to put the comma.

Making Lists

A list of words needs a comma to separate each word from the next, so that:

fish

eggs

potato chips

becomes fish, eggs, and potato chips. The second comma before the word *and* is optional.

However, if the last two items on your list could be confusing, it is best to add a comma, just in case:

I'd like eggs, potato chips, chocolate cake and fish.

Chocolate fish would probably be disgusting—add a comma and it becomes much clearer:

I'd like eggs, potato chips, chocolate cake, and fish.

It's up to you whether you think a comma is necessary or not—it also depends on what you want to end up eating.

List Extras

The items on your list don't have to be nouns. You can also make lists of adjectives, such as *fishy* and *eggy*, or verbs, such as *to eat* and *to drink;* in each case, use commas as described above.

Commas can also be used to list groups of words as well as single words. For example:

Today my baby brother scribbled on the kitchen wall, put the cat in the washing machine, broke my baseball bat, and fell asleep in the laundry basket.

Commas for Joining

When you join clauses (see pages 45–54), you usually need to put a comma in between them, like this:

My sister likes Hannah, who giggles a lot more than I do.

However, when a clause or phrase gives extra information, you need to put a comma on either side of it to split it from the rest of the sentence:

My sister likes Hannah, who giggles, a lot more than I do.

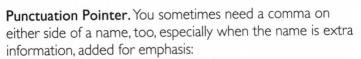

The additional information between the commas gives extra detail or adds emphasis—you could easily leave out the words inside the commas, and the sentence would still be complete. However, the meaning of the second sentence is slightly different from the meaning of the first sentence.

The first sentence says that Hannah giggles more than you and that your sister likes her. The second sentence says that Hannah giggles, but you don't like her as much as your sister does (maybe you find her giggle annoying).

Punctuation Pointer. You sometimes need a comma on either side of a name, too, especially when the name is extra information, added for emphasis:

I, Tarquin Montmorency-Futterbungle, am nine years old.
Tell me, Tarquin, are you ever teased about your name?

PUT IT IN A LETTER

Letter writing is a useful skill, regardless if it's a casual note to a friend or a cover letter for a job. And the same rules hold whether you're sending electronically or through the post office.

Addresses

Start by writing your address and the date at the top of the page on the left.

Letter Writing

Start your letter a few lines below the address and date on the left. Use "Dear," then the name of the person you are writing to, with "Mr.", "Mrs.", "Ms." or "Miss" (unless you are friends, in which case you can use their first name, of course). Add a comma after the name.

Explain what you are writing about in the first paragraph, then go into more detail in the second paragraph. Finally, finish your letter off by summarizing what you've said, and sign off with "Sincerely," followed by a comma, with your signature underneath.

A Paragraph on Paragraphs

To make your writing easier to read, break your content into paragraphs. Each one should be a group of related sentences, and you should start a new paragraph when there is a change of subject. Leave either a space between paragraphs, as in this book, or indent, which means that you start the first line of each paragraph slightly farther in from the left to show where it begins.

Old Ford Road
Anywhere, TX 20341
April 1, 2011

Dear Mrs. Brown,

I am writing in response to your advertisement for a babysitter. My name is Lucy Smith, and I am 13 years old. I have experience taking care of small children (my baby brother is 5), and I have just completed the Red Cross Babysitting Course. I am also an honor student at the Jacob Banks Middle School.

I would be happy to meet with you to learn more about the job. You may reach me by calling (444) 777-0004 or via e-mail: Lucysmith@abe.com.

Sincerely,

Lucy Smith

PUNCTUATING SPEECH

If you are writing a story and using the exact words that someone is saying, it's known as direct speech.

Quotations indicate someone's speech, and they always come in pairs. You put them around the words that are spoken.

Setting out Speech

Direct speech can be placed at the beginning, the end, or even interrupted in the middle of a sentence.

At the Beginning. When the speech comes at the beginning of a sentence, before the person who it is attributed to, you need a comma inside the quotation marks. The comma tells you the speech is finished, and you should take a small pause:

"I want to learn the trombone," said Lauren.

At the End. When the speech finished off the sentence, you need to put a comma before the quotation marks. The comma tells you the speech is about to begin, and you should take a small pause:

Lauren said, "I want to learn the trombone."

Interrupted. You can break things up a little bit by interrupting a sentence of direct speech. To do this, you need a comma inside the first set of quotation marks and another comma before the second set. In this case you don't need to start the second part of the sentence with a capital letter because it is a continuation:

"I want," said Lauren, "to learn the trombone."

However, more often than not, you will be able to split the direct speech into two separate sentences. For example:

"I love the trombone," said Lauren. "I want to learn it."

This means that in most cases, you will need to start the next part of the of speech with a capital letter.

Let's Chat

When you are writing a conversation between two or more people, you need to start a new paragraph each time a different person speaks, like this:

"Listening to Lauren's trombone," said Davindra, "is making my ears ache."

"I think she needs more practice," agreed Jack.

Punctuation Pointer. If the speech needs a question or an exclamation point, you use them in place of a comma or a period, inside the quotation marks:

"Has she stopped?" Jack asked. Davindra nodded. "At last!"

Indirect Speech

Instead of writing down the exact words that someone is saying, you can describe what they say without using quotation marks at all. This is called indirect speech:

Dermot said his favorite food is mashed potatoes.

Indirect speech is useful for factual writing, but if you're telling a story, direct speech is more fun to read—and you can get away with being a lot more casual:

"What's up?" he said.
He asked me what was up.

Which do you prefer?

Quotation Mark Extras

You can use quotation marks in your writing for lots of other things, too:

Quoting. Sometimes, especially in schoolwork, you might need to copy or quote the exact words from a book or newspaper article to support a point you're making. Put the words you quote in quotation marks to show that they're not your own:

As Penny Pincher says, "It is never the right time to ask for a pocket money raise."

Names. When you are writing by hand, use quotation marks if you mention the exact name of something, such as a book, film, play, newspaper, song, or TV program, like this:

During the weekend I watched "Junior Supercook" on TV. Then I finished my book, "Storm Island."

When you are writing on a computer, however, you should put these categories of words in *italics*.

Special Words. Sometimes it helps to use quotation marks to highlight a particular word, like this:

> If you "sequester" something, it means that you confiscate it.

Being Sarcastic. You can be sarcastic and funny about a word by putting quotation marks around it:

> My sister's "gorgeous" boyfriend is really boring.

The quotation marks show you don't agree at all with the true definition of the word. However, remember that some people don't find sarcasm very funny or clever, so they may not appreciate it (especially your sister's boyfriend)!

Double Trouble. Some sentences need two sets of quotation marks. If that happens, use single marks inside double marks, like this:

> "My favorite poem is 'Daffodils' by William Wordsworth," said Jill.

SUPERCOMMA!

The semicolon (**;**) is a very handy bit of punctuation—it's like a supercomma. Semicolons indicate a longer pause than a comma; it also indicates a smaller pause than a period.

A Balancing Act

Use a semicolon when you have two sentences that are linked to each other but don't seem strong enough to stand alone. They should be equally important, and must be talking about the same thing. For example:

> One juggler was astonishingly skillful; the other juggler was astoundingly clumsy.

Imagine your sentences sitting on either end of a seesaw. If the seesaw balances, bring in a supercomma.

Semicolon Lists

Use semicolons to make long and complicated lists easier to read, especially if there are commas separating items:

> In my backpack I stuffed lots of spare clothes in case it rained; some fruit, chocolates, and cookies; stamps and a pen; and a photo of my cat, Norman.

When each item on the list is several words long—lots of spare clothes, some chocolates, and cookies, and so on—it is much clearer to separate them with semicolons.

Punctuation Pointer. Semicolons take the place of conjunctions, words such as *or, and, but,* and *nor:*

> My brother and I were going to the park, and we planned a great day.
>
> My brother and I were going to the park; we planned a great day.

But words such as *however, nevertheless, otherwise,* and *therefore* work well following a semicolon:

> I decided to grab my raincoat before I walked out the door; otherwise, I was sure to get drenched.
>
> The clowns were extremely tired; however, they were determined to finish their performance.

Note also that there's no need for a capital letter following a semicolon.

CONQUERING COLONS

Think of the colon (**:**) as a door that opens to some new information. It lays an important role for both emphasis and clarity and is therefore ideal for introducing an explanation, a list, or a quotation.

A List

Whether the information in a list is run into a sentence or separated, a colon is a great way to introduce it:

> For the school trip to the Viking Museum, you will need: notepad, lunch, pens, and warm clothing.

> The town hall meeting will feature the following speakers:
> the mayor
> the chief of police
> the fire chief
> the chair of the town council

An explanation

Use a colon before an explanation that is preceded by a clause that can stand by itself.

> There is only one more thing to do before catching my plane: cancel the mail.

Speech and Quotations

Use a colon instead of a comma before speech, like this:

Jack said: "Since it's my birthday, I'd really like a special souvenir from the museum."

You can also use a colon to introduce a quote, like this:

As the tour guide said: "There's no reason for anyone to be wearing any of the exhibits when they leave."

Punctuation Pointer. There are also times when you don't use the colon, such as after the words, *included, were,* and *was.*

The recipe included eggs, sugar, and flour.

Her favorite author is J. K. Rowling.

124

APOSTROPHE ALERT

Just remember one simple rule: There are only two reasons you ever need an apostrophe (**'**). One is to indicate the possessive—it shows that something belongs. The other shows omission—that letters have been left out. Here's how they work:

One Careful Owner

When you see an apostrophe and a letter **s** at the end of a word, it shows that something belongs to that word, as in:

The cat's pajamas (the pajamas belonging to the cat)

and

The bee's knees (the knees of the bee)

This rule works for any singular owner. It could be a cat or a bee, or a person or an object, like this:

Jack's book
The book's cover

If a word ends in a letter **s** already, you still need to add on the **s** after the apostrophe. For example:

The princess's slippers

Rule Breakers

If the end of a name is pronounced "iz" or "eez," you shouldn't add the extra **s** after the apostrophe—it sounds strange if you do! Examples of words like these include the names Sophocles (pronounced SOF-o-kleez) and Archimedes (pronounced ark-i-MEED-eez). Write them like this:

Sophocles' plays

Archimedes' inventions

These examples all show possession for singular nouns, but the rules work slightly differently for plurals.

More Than One Owner

When the owner is plural—the boys, the girls, the cats, or the bees, for example—the apostrophe goes after the **s:**

That is the boys' dinner (the dinner belongs to two or more boys).

If a plural, such as *children, men,* or *mice* doesn't end in an **s,** you need to add an apostrophe and an **s,** like this:

the children's playground

the men's ears

the mice's cheese

Punctuation Pointer. Remember, it makes no difference whether the thing that belongs is singular or plural. Only look at whether the owner is singular or plural to decide where the apostrophe goes.

Vanishing Letters

A contraction, when letters are omitted, is something that you use particularly when you are talking. It makes a word shorter and quicker to say. *Aren't,* for example, is short for *are not*—the two words are joined together, and the **o** in *not* is removed. An apostrophe is put in place of the **o** to show that it has been removed.

The letter **o** is one of the most common vanishing letters. Here are some more examples:

In Full	Contraction
cannot	can't
could not	couldn't
did not	didn't
do not	don't
had not	hadn't
has not	hasn't
is not	isn't
should not	shouldn't
were not	weren't
would not	wouldn't

Rule Breakers

The following two examples are shortened differently:

shall not	shan't
will not	won't

Did You Know?

There is an apostrophe in a word that you use every day, whatever time it is—*o'clock*. Here, "of the clock," meaning "according to the clock," has been shortened.

Common Confusions

The words listed below sound the same but mean different things. Ask yourself if your sentence has *is* or *are* in it, from the verb to be, and you'll know that the word needs an apostrophe to replace the missing letter. Here are some examples:

it's (it is)
It's time for bed.

its (possessive)
The baby wants *its* bed.

there's (there is)
There's a fishing boat.

theirs (possessive)
Theirs is a blue boat.

who's (who is)
Who's going to the park?

whose (possessive)
Whose shoes are these?

you're (you are)
You're boring me.

your (possessive)
Your nose has a spot on it.

Punctuation Pointer. The possessive nouns *hers, his, ours, theirs, yours*—just like *its*—these possessive pronouns don't need apostrophes. See page 19 for more on possessive pronouns.

Quick Checklist

Each part of the verbs *to be* and *to have* can be shortened in the present tense using an apostrophe:

To Be		**To Have**	
I am	I'm	I have	I've
you are	you're	you have	you've
he is	he's	he has	he's
she is	she's	she has	she's
it is	it's	it has	it's
we are	we're	we have	we've
you are	you're	you have	you've
they are	they're	they have	they've

Punctuation Pointer. In the future tense (see pages 29 and 30) you use the auxiliary verb *will.* This is often shortened to 'll—as in *I'll, you'll, she'll, they'll,* and so on.

'70s Or 1970s?

Apostrophes can be used with numbers to show possession or omission, but never to make a plural. Writing about music *of* the 1970s, you might say:

> The 1970s' songs my dad loves are really weird.

However, it is more acceptable to use 1970s.

If you are just writing about the 1970s decade, you can shorten it to '70s with an apostrophe:

> The '70s had lots of weird music my dad loves.

PARENTHESES

Parentheses always come in pairs **(**like this**)**. You use them to isolate one part of the sentence from the rest.

You can use them to explain things, to give opinions, and to make an interruption:

> Giraffes are very tall (giants are taller) with long necks.

The useful thing about parentheses is that stuff inside them is kept totally separate from the rest of the sentence, which doesn't happen when you use commas:

> Giraffes are very tall, giants are taller, with long necks.

Punctuating Parentheses

If the words inside your parentheses are a whole sentence, rather than appearing in the middle of a sentence, you should put the period inside the parentheses, like this:

> My teenage brother is still asleep. (He's been asleep all day.) It's possible he's been enchanted.

If your sentence has a comma in it, place the words in parentheses with the part of the sentence they belong to:

> I wanted a doughnut (the oozy, yummy kind), but Mom gave me an apple instead.

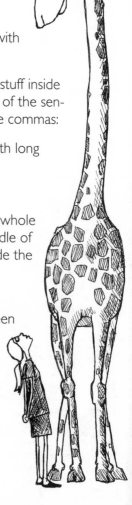

DASHES AND HYPHENS

Dashes (–) are a useful replacement for other types of punctuation, as long as you don't overuse them.

Single Dash

Single dashes can work like commas, semicolons, or colons:

I eat fruit almost every day—but I never eat fish.

You can use them to add a bit of suspense or emotion to your writing, like this:

I turned the corner and suddenly there I found—my missing cat!

You can even let speech tail away with a dash, for example:

"I like the new girl, but—" said Emily uncertainly.

Double Dashes

Double dashes work a little like parentheses and separate one part of a sentence from the rest, like this:

Humpty Dumpty—silly thing—fell off the wall.

How to Hyphenate

Hyphens (-) look like dashes, but they are shorter. However, instead of separating, they join two or more words together to make new words. These are called compound words. The hyphens show that the joined words belong to each other:

son-in-law
green-eyed monster
ten-pound baby

You don't have to use a hyphen for all compound words, but always add one if you think it makes things clearer, especially if the compound word precedes a noun:

a low-budget job

a first class decision

Punctuation Pointer. Do not use hyphens in words that are preceded by "un-," "anti-," "pre-," "post-" and "co-," such as *coworker* and *postwar*. Check your dictionary first.

When to Use Hyphens

Use a hyphen if you think your meaning would be unclear without one. For example, it would be easy to misunderstand who was eating who in this sentence:

Beware! Man eating crocodiles!

This is much clearer:

Beware! Man-eating crocodiles!

Hyphens and Numbers

When you are writing out numbers and fractions that are more than one word, you'll need hyphens. For instance, ⅘ becomes *four-fifths* and 24 becomes *twenty-four.* Don't go wild, though—it's *five hundred and forty-eight,* not *five-hundred-and-forty-eight.*

When combining two or more words with a number to form a compound adjective in front of a noun, you must use hyphens:

A 20-foot pole

An 18-inch television set

A 12-hour shift

But if the number phrase is not modifying a noun, hyphens are not necessary:

The bag of potatoes weighs five pounds.

Three hours later we went to the movies.

The field was 400 feet wide.

COUNT ON CAPITALS

You know that you need a capital letter at the beginning of a sentence, but there are other times you use a capital letter, too (see Proper Nouns, page 15). Use the checklist below to help you put them in the right place.

Punctuation Pointer. When you are writing about yourself, *I* is always a capital letter—*me* and *my* are not.

Capitals Checklist

Names of People. Always use a capital with names (such as Millie or Jacob), surnames (such as Milton or Jones), and titles (such as Miss and Mr., or President or Sir):

> Miss Millie Milton
> Mr. Jacob Jones
> President Smith
> Sir Montague Ponsonby-Smythe

Sometimes titles need a mix of capital and lowercase letters. If you are writing about the President of the United States, for example, *of* and *the* don't need capital letters, but the words President and United States do. However, if you are writing about presidents in general, rather than a particular president, there's no need for a capital letter.

The same rule applies to prime ministers, royalty, and other important people, too.

Titles. Always use capitals for the titles of films, plays, books, and TV programs, like this:

The Wizard of Oz
Romeo and Juliet
The Secret Garden
Sesame Street

Notice that, in these cases, you *should* capitalize *The* because it is included in the actual titles.

Place Names. The names of places—whether they are the town where you were born, the country you live in, or the name of a river or mountain—should be capitalized as well.

Here are some examples:

Phoenix
United States
Mississippi
Mt. Ranier

Some words, such as *north, south, east,* and *west,* are usually lowercase, unless they're part of a name—for example, the North Pole and South Korea.

Religious Words. The names of religions, such as *Judaism, Christianity, Islam,* and *Buddhism,* all need a capital letter at the beginning. And *God, Allah, Buddha,* and other religious names need capital letters, too.

Dates or Special Days. The names of days, months, and festivals or special holidays all need an initial capital letter.

History. If you are writing about events in history, such as the First World War, the Middle Ages, or the Battle of Waterloo— you guessed it—call in the capitals!

And Finally...

One last bit of advice, now that you've read about the rules of grammar, spelling, and punctuation: Keep practicing. When you put your knowledge about how to WRITE into practice— whether you're composing a prizewinning poem, writing a thank-you letter to a relative, or entering a short-story competition—you'll be sure to get things RIGHT!

INDEX

A

"a" or "an" *see* indefinite article 15

abbreviations 105–6, 109

abstract nouns 16–17

acronyms 107

active voice 58

addresses 115

adjectives 14, 23–5

   clauses as 55

   comparative 23

   phrases as 56–7

   superlative 24–5

adverbs 14, 40–2

   clauses as 55

   phrases as 57

agreement 53

allegory 61

alliteration 9, 61

alphabet 70, 79

anagrams 98

"and" *see also* coordinating
   conjunctions 45–6

antonyms 63

apostrophes 125–29

apostrophe checklist 129

articles 15

assonance 61

auxiliary verbs
   "to be" and "to have" 31

B

"be" *see also* auxiliary verbs 31

"but" *see also* coordinating
   conjunctions 45–6

C

c, hard and soft sound 76, 96

capital letters 104, 107, 134–37

Caribbean language words 69

clauses 54–5

   as nouns 55

   as adjectives 55

   as adverbs 55

   main 54

   subordinate 47, 54

clichés 62

collective nouns 17

colons 123–24

commas 112–14

common nouns 15

comparative adjectives 23–5,

compound conjunctions 47

compound words 131–32

conjunctions 14, 45–7

   compound 47

   coordinating 45

correlative 47
subordinate 47
consonants 70, 75–7
double 77
hard and soft 76
consonant checker 75
contractions 106
coordinating conjunctions 45–7
correlative conjunctions 47

D
dashes 131–33
definite article 15
dictionaries 28, 79–80
diphthongs 72
direct questions 108
direct speech 117

E
"–ed" see past participles
Einstein, Albert 78
exclamations 41
exclamation marks 14, 108–11, 118

F
French words 69
future tense 30, 35–6

G
g, hard and soft sound 76, 96,

H
hard c and g 76, 96
"have" see also auxiliary verbs 31
heteronyms 89
homographs 89
homophones 88
hyperbole 62
hyphens 131–33

I
i before e 72
indefinite article 15
indirect questions 109
indirect speech 119
infinitives 27
split 64
"–ing" see present participle 32, 33
"–ing" adjectives 50
"–ing" nouns 49
"–ing" suffix 50
interjections 14, 48
interrobang 111
Inuit language words 69
invasions 68–9
irregular participles 39
irregular verbs 38–9
irregular verb table 39

L

Latin words 68
letter writing 115–16
letters, silent 80–1

M

magic e 71
main clauses 54–5
metaphors 62

N

names 83, 114, 115, 119, 134–37
new words 64, 90, 131
Norse words 68
nouns 15–17
  abstract 16
  clauses as 55
  collective 17, 53
  common 15, 16
  object 27, 52, 55, 59
  phrases as 56
  proper 16
  subject 52, 53, 55, 56
  verbal 49
numbers 106, 129, 133

O

object nouns 27, 52, 55, 59
object pronouns 19
"of" 10, 44
omission 125, 129

onomatopoeia 88–90
opposite meanings 27, 63, 87
ordering words 58–9
oxymorons 62

P

palindromes 98
paradox 62
paragraphs 115
parentheses 130
participles 32–4
  past participles 34, 38–9
  present participle 32–3
parts of speech, the 14
adjectives 23–5
  adverbs 40–2
  conjunctions 45–7
  interjections 48
  nouns 15–17
  prepositions 43–4, 50, 64
  pronouns 18–22
  verbs 26–9
passive voice 58
past participles 33
past perfect tense 34
past tense 33–4
personification 63
phrases 56–7
  as adjectives 56–7
  as adverbs 57
  as nouns 56
place names 135–37
plurals 82–5

possession 126–29

possessive pronouns 19, 126

prefixes 86–7

prefix checklist 86

prepositions 43–4, 50, 64

present participle 32–3

present tense 32–3, 38–9, 129

pronouns 18–22

   object 19

   possessive 18

   reflexive 21

   relative 21

   subject 19

proper nouns 16

punctuation 101–137

   abbreviations 105, 107

   apostrophes 125–129

   capital letters 134

   colons 123

   commas 112–114

   contractions 106

   dashes 131

   exclamation points 109

   period 104–107, 118, 130

   hyphens 131–133

   question marks 108–109

   semicolons 121–122

Q

questions 108–9

   direct 108

   indirect 109

question marks 108–9

quotation marks 117–120

R

reflexive pronouns 21–22

regular verbs 38

relative pronouns 21

religious words 136

S

sarcasm 120

semicolons 121–122

sentences 51–53

   object nouns 27

   subject nouns 27, 58

"shall" *see also* auxiliary verbs

silent letters 80–81

similes 63

singular words 53, 85, 125–26

   and apostrophes 125

   soft c and g 76

speech 117–120

   direct 117

   indirect 119

speech, the parts of 14–29

   see also parts of speech

split digraph 71

split infinitives 64

spoonerisms 99

subject nouns 52

subject pronouns 19

subordinate clauses 54–5
subordinate conjunctions 47
suffixes 77
supercomma, see semicolons
superlative adjectives 23
syllables 71
synonyms 63

T
tautology 63
tenses 30–7
  future 35–7
  past 33–4
  past perfect 34
  present 30–3
  thesaurus 28
"the" see definite article

V
verbal nouns 49
verbs 14, 26–39
  auxiliary 36–7
  irregular 39
  regular 38
  tense 31–7
voice 58
vowels 71–4
vowel checker 73–4

W
"will" see *also* auxiliary verbs
word order 59–60
writing style 59–65
  adding speech 60
  allegory 61
  alliteration 61
  antonyms 63
  assonance 61
  bad grammar 64
  clichés 62
  hyperbole 62
  metaphors 62
  oxymorons 62
  paradox 62
  personification 63
  similes 63
  synonyms 63
  tautology 63